Fly Fishing the Yellowstone in the Park

GREYCLIFF RIVER BOOK SERIES

Volume 4

For my Friend Dolph:
who shares my love of
wild rivers and streams, Trout,
the F.F.F., Fly Fishing,
and of course,
The Yellowstone

Bob Jacklin
8/13/01

Fly Fishing the Yellowstone in the Park

by Bob Jacklin and Gary LaFontaine

Greycliff Publishing Company

Helena, Montana

Cover photographs:
Lower Falls, Grand Canyon of the Yellowstone, © Stan Bradshaw
Inset: Yellowstone River, © Bob Jacklin

Frontispiece: Sharyn Jacklin nets a cutthroat just above the Cascade picnic area on the Yellowstone River.

Book photographs: Unless otherwise noted all photographs are © Bob Jacklin

Fly photographs by Doug O'looney

Copyright © 2001 by Bob Jacklin and Gary LaFontaine
All rights reserved.

Printed in the United States of America.

No part of this book may be used or reproduced in any manner whatsoever without written permission except in the case of brief quotations embodied in critical articles or reviews. For information, address Greycliff Publishing Company, P.O. Box 1273, Helena, MT 59624.

Designed and typeset in Cyanide Gothic, Giovanni, ITC Benguiat Gothic, and Lucida Handwriting by Marcy Chovanak, Greycliff Publishing Company, Helena, Montana

Cover design by Geoff Wyatt, Helena, Montana

Printed by Advanced Litho Printing, Great Falls, Montana

11 10 09 08 07 06 05 04 03 02 01 12 11 10 9 8 7 6 5 4 3 2 1

Library of Congress Cataloging-in-Publication Data

Jacklin, Bob, 1945–
Fly fishing the Yellowstone in the park / by Bob Jacklin and Gary LaFontaine.
p. cm. — (Greycliff River book series ; v. 4)
Includes bibliographical references (p.).
ISBN 1-890373-10-9 (alk. paper)
1. Fly fishing—Yellowstone National Park. 2. Fly fishing—Yellowstone River.
I. LaFontaine, Gary. II. Title. III. Series.
SH464.Y45 J23 2001
799.1'24'0978752—dc21 2001023634

To all those who have gone before me who have shared this kinship in trout, wild rivers, and of course the Yellowstone.

For my dad, who has shared this great fishery and many great experiences with me in Yellowstone.

Contents

ILLUSTRATIONS

Preface
by Gary LaFontaine

This book started out as several hours of recorded interview between its authors—more of a conversation, really, that took advantage of two persons' combined experience on the Yellowstone River in Yellowstone National Park. Bob brings more than thirty years' experience as an outfitter and guide in the greater Yellowstone area, most especially on the upper Yellowstone in the Park.

Though not as continuously, I have fished the upper Yellowstone for twenty-plus years and, during the mid-1980s, I guided out of West Yellowstone for four years. Many of my days with clients were spent on various rivers inside and outside Yellowstone Park—the Madison, Gallatin, Firehole, Lamar, Gardner, and Slough Creek. My favorite river for teaching people how to fly fish, however, was the Yellowstone River inside the Park. It was then—as it is now—the perfect place for studying the reactions of wild trout.

Occasionally someone would say, "Those Yellowstone cutthroats are dumb."

I loved to take people up to the river early in the season, right after opening day. That's when the fishing was easy. All the trout had come downstream from Yellowstone Lake to spawn, and now they were heading back upstream. They were hungry, totally unwise to the ways of the river, and unnaturally overpopulated during this migration. It was these spawners, these lake fish, that gave the river the reputation for having "dumb" trout.

I also loved to take people up to the river later in the season. By late July the spawning fish had returned to the lake, and only the resident fish were left in the river. Suddenly, there were no more "dumb" trout. The Yellowstone River could be as tough as the Henry's Fork or Silver Creek on their fussiest days. The same people who called the fish in the Yellowstone stupid were getting refusals to size-20 dry flies on 6X tippets.

Many times Bob Jacklin and I have sat and talked about those "tough" days on the river. We both love to teach people how to fly fish—what can be better than to stand next to a student on the Yellowstone watching a 20-inch cutthroat come ever-so-slowly up through the clear water to nose a tiny Foam Ant? We love the river because we know we will get chance after chance with wild trout. We love the river because we know it in all its moods.

Making the audio tape together was tremendous fun because we understand what makes the Yellowstone both easy and difficult. And we understand how to fish it when it is easy and when it is difficult. For me the enjoyment was enhanced by the tremendous depth of Bob Jacklin's experience and knowledge, but more than that, it was really magnified by his great passion for the river. This man really loves the Yellowstone.

The question and answer format of the two-day recording session, captured and presented in the acclaimed audio tape, *Fly Fishing the Yellowstone in the Park,* is transformed and updated here into book form. It is presented in a single voice, Bob's, though, obviously, there were two voices and give and take recorded throughout the session.

There was also a third "voice" not actually heard in the audio tape—the voice calling suggestions from the other room, the voice making us go over a particular point two and three times until we got it right, and finally the voice that belonged to the hand and mind that cut and spliced the eight hours of raw tape into an easy-listening, ninety-minute format. That voice belonged to project editor Stan Bradshaw—he was our intellectual guide.

This book reads so well because it is such tight copy. The three of us: Bob, Stan, and I, created the audio version and it is because this written version started as an audio tape that it is such a fast-paced, information-packed book on the Yellowstone.

The credit for really knowing the Yellowstone in the Park goes to Bob. He was amazing. Often, during the taping session, I wanted to reach for pad and pencil to make notes while he was talking. Then, I would remember that I didn't have to write down his words, that everything was being recorded. Still, there were many moments when I wished that his ideas were down on paper. Now they are.

Finally, I learned about more than the Yellowstone from Bob Jacklin. I learned a lot about fly fishing. So will you. And you will enjoy reading about a great trout river.

THE YELLOWSTONE RIVER

of Yellowstone National Park

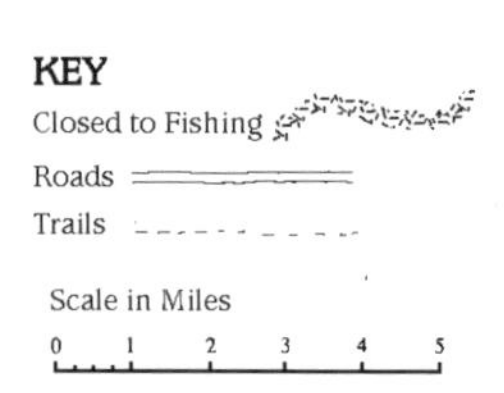

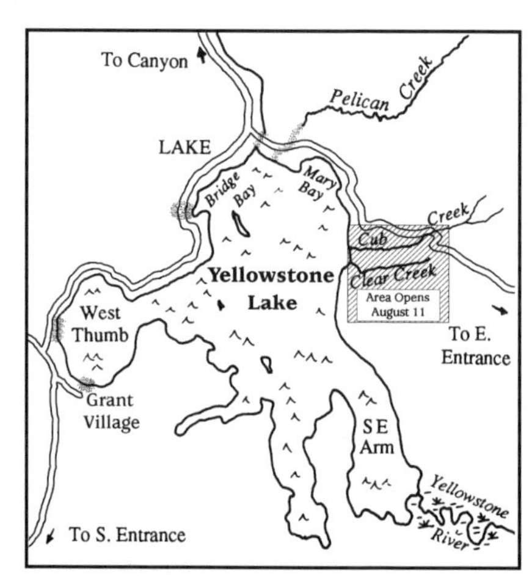

SECTIONS

For information on Yellowstone Park fishing licenses and regulations, contact

Yellowstone National Park
P.O. Box 168
Yellowstone National Park, WY 82190-0168
Visitor Information (307) 344-7381 Fax (307) 344-2005
TDD (307) 344-2386
e-mail: yell_visitor_services@nps.gov http://www.nps.gov/yell

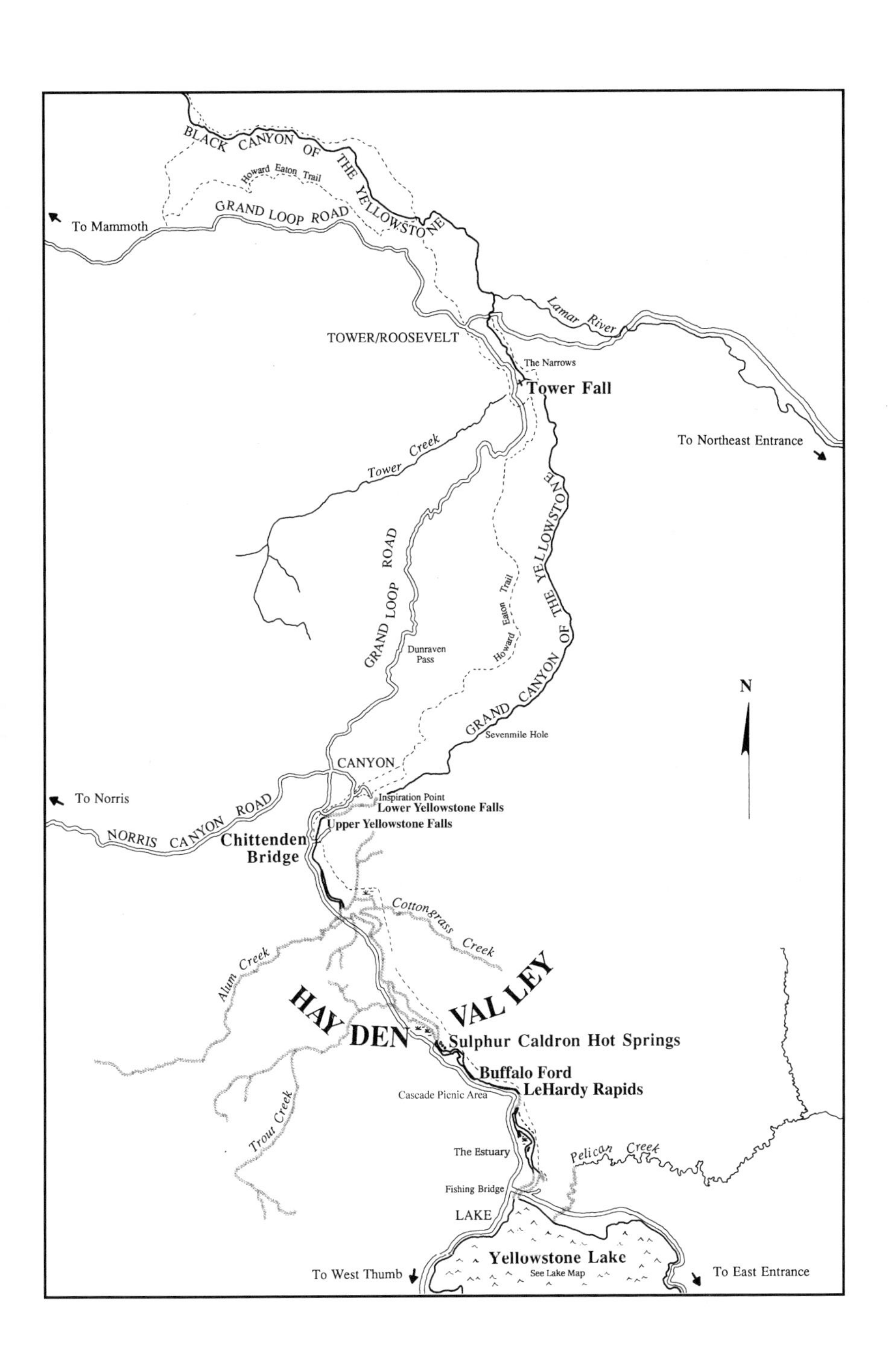
BLACK CANYON OF THE YELLOWSTONE
Howard Eaton Trail
GRAND LOOP ROAD
To Mammoth
Lamar River
TOWER/ROOSEVELT
The Narrows
Tower Fall
To Northeast Entrance
Tower Creek
GRAND LOOP ROAD
GRAND CANYON OF THE YELLOWSTONE
Howard Eaton Trail
Dunraven Pass
N
Sevenmile Hole
CANYON
To Norris
NORRIS CANYON ROAD
Inspiration Point
Lower Yellowstone Falls
Upper Yellowstone Falls
Chittenden Bridge
Cottongrass Creek
Alum Creek
HAYDEN VALLEY
Sulphur Caldron Hot Springs
Buffalo Ford
LeHardy Rapids
Cascade Picnic Area
Trout Creek
The Estuary
Pelican Creek
Fishing Bridge
LAKE
Yellowstone Lake
See Lake Map
To West Thumb
To East Entrance

The Yellowstone Blackspotted Cutthroat is a unique strain of cutthroat trout indigenous only to the Yellowstone drainage. This specimen shows the species' distinctive large black spots located primarily on the back half of the fish. Its head and dorsal area are medium olive; the body is slightly gold; the gill plate is deep violet-red. The tail and fins are dark olive to deep red. Under the lower jaw, the trout exhibits the bright crimson slash that earned its name.

(Photo by Sharyn Jacklin)

Introduction

There really isn't another trout fishery in this entire country—and maybe in the world—like the Yellowstone River. The Yellowstone has been there since long before any recorded history. The Indians likely visited, as did Lewis and Clark, John Colter, and other early explorers. The fish—a wild strain of the Yellowstone Blackspotted Cutthroat—were there then. The journals of Lewis and Clark mentioned finding them. The cutthroats that Lewis and Clark encountered averaged about three pounds.

These Yellowstone cutthroats are big, and they live in clear water. It's like going into Labrador a hundred years ago and finding a stream of wild brook trout. Only here, anyone in the nation could drive right up to its bank and experience the same thing.

There's a general perception that the Yellowstone cutthroat is a real chump, an easy fish to catch. That perception is only true part of the time. The fish that you encounter right after season opening is most likely to be a lake cutthroat and not a river fish. Right after the season opening, the fish is a chump because it's hungry. It spent the better part of a year in Yellowstone Lake. It worked its way downstream to spawn. It's just finished spawning, the water temperature warms up slightly, and it starts feeding like crazy. After months of relative scarcity, it finds a smorgasbord of food in the river in early July.

The lake cutthroats spend the rest of the summer feeding and eventually working back up toward Yellowstone Lake again. You can usually tell the lake-bred trout from the river trout. The resident trout are in good shape; they look good and they might be a little larger because they feed better. The lake fish are not really that good looking. They're a little thin, they're spawned out, and it takes them another month or two before they start filling out.

In the late season, when the lake fish move back out of the river, the fishing gets much harder. I've had some very tough days there. From the latter part of August and into October, a couple of fish per day may be all you can get.

From the time of Lewis and Clark, all the way into the early years of the Park's creation, the fishery was unbelievably prolific. There are hundreds of photographs of people with stringers of twenty-five to fifty to a hundred trout. They would catch them to supply the dining facilities at Old Faithful and other areas around the Park. But many of the fish caught—numbering into the thousands per year, simply ended up in Park trash cans.

Shortly after the middle of the twentieth century—certainly by the early sixties—the fishery appeared to be in decline. For a kid like me, coming from New Jersey, it still seemed pretty darned good fishing—there seemed to be plenty of big fish, and plenty of great hatches. But too many anglers were keeping a limit of fish and it was beginning to take its toll on the fishery. With the support of the fly-fishing community, Yellowstone National Park enacted a "fish-for-fun" regulation for the upper Yellowstone River above Yellowstone Falls. The new regulation, which went into effect in 1968, was among the first catch-and-release regulations in the United States.

Within a year or two after the regulations went into effect, we saw a lot more fish in the river. Not only have the numbers improved, but the size of the fish has increased until today an honest average measured size would be about 16 to 18 inches, somewhere between a pound and a

The upper Yellowstone River in the Park is designated as catch and release and is well posted. The attitude of anglers in the Park, as well as Park regulations, has been a major factor in keeping this one of the finest wild fisheries in the lower forty-eight states. Check Yellowstone National Park fishing regulations for other rules pertaining to the upper Yellowstone, its tributaries, and other Park waters.

pound and a half. Still, these fish are likely not as big as those witnessed by Lewis and Clark. They top out about 20—occasionally 22—inches. Nevertheless, the cutthroat fishery in Yellowstone River in the Park, today ranks as one of the great wild trout fisheries in the world.

Twenty miles long, fourteen miles wide, and 400 feet deep, Yellowstone Lake is America's largest mountain lake. Fishing its shore is like fishing a small ocean. When the wind is up, the wave action stirs up food from the bottom and fish move close to shore to feed.

Chapter 1

Sections of the River

SURF FISHING ON YELLOWSTONE LAKE

Yellowstone Lake is one of the largest alpine lakes in the world. By alpine, I mean a lake that is over 7,000 feet in elevation. The ice usually comes off around about June 10 or so, and the lake stays ice cold pretty much all year. That water is so cold that it scares me. You don't want to go overboard in the middle of the lake. You have to use some good judgment when you're boating on the lake, or fishing and wading the lake. Just a few minutes in that water is enough to kill you with hypothermia. Add wind and waves to those ice cold temperatures and you have a lake that can be really dangerous if you're not careful. Wind and storms normally come up from the west, but they can come up from any direction, and then it really gets rough. It's like fishing the Atlantic Ocean.

From the standpoint of successfully fishing the lake, you don't need to be out in the middle of the lake. Your best fishing is going to be along the shoreline. As large lakes go, Yellowstone Lake is quite barren. The primary food species are plankton and some insect life, and those creatures will be more concentrated along the shoreline, in the littoral zone, than in the middle of the lake.

This is both good news and bad news for the angler. The good part is that the fish are hungry in the lake. The bad news is the water's cold and you have to get the fly down to them, so this means fishing a sinking line or a sink-tip line. The water can be 10 to 12 feet deep right off shore. But leave your lead weights at home. Leaded fishing tackle—leaded split shot, weighted jigs (lead molded to a hook), and soft lead-weighted ribbon—are prohibited in Yellowstone Park. There are tin and bismuth substitutes which will work equally well.

Fortunately, these fish are hungry enough to be indiscriminate in their feeding. Instinctively they will take anything down deep that moves. The key to success is to get your fly down. Try to find a spot where fish are concentrated. The fish tend to be evenly distributed all along the shoreline of Yellowstone Lake, especially when it first opens June 15 each year. But the bays and the mouths of creeks are places fish start staging for spawning, and those areas tend to have more fish.

There are a number of tributaries whose mouths are accessible along the lake shore. The first stream that comes to mind is Pelican Creek, the lower reaches of which are closed to fishing. Also, Clear Creek and Cub Creek are a nice walk from the east entrance road of the Park. As you come into the Park from the east, the first time you hit the lake, there's a trailhead right in that area that takes off south toward those two tributaries.

Each year during spring spawning, thousands of cutthroat trout enter Cub Creek, one of the main spawning tributaries of Yellowstone Lake. Note the school of cutthroats that has just entered the mouth of Cub Creek (at bottom of photo).

Once you get to there, park regulations require that you not fish any closer to the mouth of a tributary than one hundred yards. But those fish will start to stage all along those shorelines. So wade out as deep as you can, cast as far as you can, and allow the line to sink toward the bottom, as fish will be down deep. Then strip your line in slowly and be alert for a soft strike.

One way to find fish is to spot them from above. There are usually high bluffs or hills along the lake and you can stand up there on a midday without too much wind and pick the fish out.

Fly patterns for this deep fishing don't have to be too sophisticated. For this early-season lake fishing, leave your dry flies home. Later in the season, fish may come up for a dry, but normally, early in the year, they'll be near the bottom. I like to use a large—size 4 or 6—Woolly Bugger with lots of flash in the tail for the early season. As the season advances, I'll go with a smaller nymph, such as a Zug Bug, Bead Head Prince Nymph, or a Hare's Ear Nymph in sizes 8 or 10. The pattern isn't too important. Use just any size 8 or 10 dark—black or gray with some peacock are good colors—as long as it has some weight and it gets down.

Another good thing about these tributaries, if the trails are open early in the year, is that you have a chance to go in and see these fish moving up the stream, in the act of spawning. Forget about fishing—the streams are closed until later in the season—the fish are in there thick, spawning, and that is really something that you should see. It is humbling to see that many fish crowded into the little tributaries, fighting to spawn. I can remember seeing anglers catching and keeping limits and over-limits of spawning trout through the sixties and seventies. Fortunately, the tributaries are now closed to all fishing throughout the spawning season.

There are a few places on the lake, little backwater areas and bays, that can have better concentrations of fish throughout the summer. I especially like Mary's Bay on the east side. It's a little bit out of the wind at times, and in the mornings there are some bluffs from which you can look down and actually pick your fish. Then you can go down and either wade out or take a small craft out there and try to catch some of these fish right off that particular point. Because it's sheltered from the wind, and it's generally shallow, it tends to be a little bit warmer than the rest of the lake. And fish, being cold-blooded, get a little more active with warmer water. So, with the warmer conditions at Mary's Bay, the fish will move farther to feed, and may even surface to take dry flies.

Another really good early-season spot is the West Thumb of Yellowstone Lake. Along the Grand Loop Road from Bluff Point to Pumice Point on the north shore of West Thumb

Bay, there are several good access points and parking areas for anglers. There is a long sandy peninsula at one of these parking areas which separates the main lake from a small back water. This sandy beach is one of my favorite early-season places to catch some of those unwelcome lake trout that have invaded the lake. These lake trout are not native to the lake, and the Park Service is anxious to reduce their numbers in order to sustain the cutthroat fishery. At ice-out, the lakers will cruise the warmer, shallow water along this beach in search of food. If you catch any of these lake trout, Park regulations require you to keep them. Even with the concentration of lake trout in this area, you'll still catch about ten cutthroats for every lake trout you catch.

One last tip on fishing Yellowstone Lake—dead calm conditions do not offer optimal fishing conditions. You are much better off with some wind and waves to stir up food along shore. It's this turbulence which brings the fish in close to feed. Watch for the mud line stirred up against the bank, and fish along the edge of that line. At its best, it feels a little like surf fishing in the ocean.

Yellowstone River above the Lake

BIG FISH IN THE BOONDOCKS

There's so much accessible water along shore next to the road that it's hard to imagine traveling all the way across Yellowstone Lake, but there can be some incredible fishing upstream of the South Arm of the lake. You can go by horseback, or backpack, or take a boat and paddle or row across. There are no motors allowed up the southeast arm of the lake, but then you can paddle up with a canoe, or hike in some of these trails, to get up to where the main Yellowstone comes in and feeds Yellowstone Lake.

The fish are no bigger upstream of the lake than they are downstream, but they haven't seen as many flies or as many people. If it's busy back here, you'll see maybe one or two other people. It's pristine country and a pleasure to fish. It's called the Back Country Area. A trip to the river above the lake is not a spur-of-the-moment thing. It's a long enough haul that, once there, you want to be able to spend a night or two.

While you're not going to catch more fish and you're not going to catch larger fish, the isolation of these fish means that they come readily to the fly. And you're not going to have a social problem with too many fishermen. For a back country spot like this, take a good supply of wet and dry flies. Have some Woolly Buggers or Bead Head Buggers with black, olive, or peacock body and a black marabou tail. Take a selection of nymphs, such as the Prince Nymph, Pheasant Tail, Hare's Ear, and the March Brown, in sizes 10 and 12. To finish your wet fly selection, take several of the old Mickey Finn Streamers or Muddlers in sizes 6 and 8. My dry-fly selection would include the Gray Wulff, Royal Wulff, Goofus Bug, Adams, Parachute Adams, Orange Double Wing, and Elk Hair Caddis, all in sizes 12, 14, and 16. For the late season, include a good supply of hopper patterns in sizes 6, 8, and 10.

The Estuary

FLAT WATER AND CHALLENGING

There are many famous dry-fly waters throughout the world. I'd put the Estuary, at the outlet of Yellowstone Lake, near the top of any list of great dry-fly waters. It's flat water, but it has just enough movement and volume to it, to make it really great for a dry fly. Its big weed beds provide plenty of cover, and harbor abundant insect life. The great width of the Estuary provides plenty of space.

The Estuary fish are fussy, in part because the fish there have a longer time to look over your offering. If you're fishing

This wide, flat section, called the Estuary, is just above the canyon where the river flows in to Le Hardy Rapids. Because the Estuary's water is slower and deeper, this area offers both good dry-fly fishing during hatches and excellent nymph fishing all season long.

a dry fly, the fish can come up and look at it at their leisure. They get a much better look at it here than they do below Le Hardy Rapids or at the Buffalo Ford area, so they tend to be a little more picky.

The key to successfully fishing the Estuary is more one of presentation and line control than of fly pattern. To be sure, there are certain occasions when trout key on specific flies, and they'll want a matching pattern, but most of the time, the important factor is whether you can achieve a drag-free float.

Flat water can be deceptively busy. While it may not be obvious to casual observation, the water will billow up over the weeds, and it'll push a fly, and it will pull on both your fly and leader until you end up with drag. So, you have to read the currents and control your line accordingly. To help my leader control, I rig specifically for this situation. My tackle is a standard butt-section and a nine foot leader with about 24 to 30 inches of tippet.

For many years, I guided an old man who used a 34-inch tippet. That extra tippet gave him a lot more freedom of float on his flies, and it paid off consistently for him. Adding that longer tippet to the end of your leader really is the key to success in dry-fly fishing, and especially so in places like the Estuary. And pay close attention to tippet size here. Most often I'll use 5X.

If you use 5X in a downstream approach, with a natural drift, you can fool just about any fish. To effectively fish downstream, cast quartering down with lots of slack line, so the fly will drift drag-free into the trout's window ahead of the leader. The downstream approach assures that you see the fish and that you exercise pinpoint control in your casting. One bad cast here can put the fish down. But if you get the cast right, the chances of inducing a strike are high.

In order to be most effective on the Estuary, I try to let my eyes do most of the fishing for me. I look for insects first, and second I look for some indication of feeding fish. Because the water is so slow here, the fish will tend to cruise instead of simply holding in one place like they might do in faster water. The fish normally will have a territory they work; they'll cruise up and back.

When I can spot a cruising fish, I'll see if I can wade myself into position to cast. Don't just cast from wherever you happen to be when you spot the fish. Take a minute and put yourself in the right place—walk or wade *carefully* into position, then make your cast. You're bound to have a lot more success than just casting from wherever you happen to be. Try to pick an approach that will minimize current drag, and that gives you the shortest possible cast. The shorter your cast, the better your ability to control drag, and the longer your drag-free floats.

This short canyon section just below the Estuary of Yellowstone Lake is a prime place to catch trout because fish move through it to reach and return from their spawning grounds downstream.

On the flat water of the Estuary, I prefer to use parachute patterns. In July a size-14 Rusty Para-Spin spinner is a good choice. In August, I like the standard Parachute Adams in sizes 14 and 16. But, because this is big water, these wild cutthroats will sometimes go for the big bite of food. If nothing else is working, a large attractor such as a Royal Wulff in size 12 sometimes will move the fish. Below the surface, I like olive and partridge soft hackle patterns in sizes 12 and 14 for the Estuary. And another good standard for the Estuary is the Emergent Sparkle Pupa in size and color to match the caddis you'll find there.

If you're really skilled at fishing small nymphs, the Estuary is good water. Patterns such as the Blackfly Larva in sizes 18 and 20, Variegated Midge Larva in sizes 18 through 26, or a Bead Head Hare's Ear in sizes 18 and 20 consistently fool fish. The best way to fish these flies is dead-drift under a strike indicator. The key to success here, again, is to avoid drag.

Le Hardy Rapids is closed to fishing because the steep banks, swift water, and rapids are too dangerous to navigate on foot, but at times in the spring you can view spawning cutthroats from the boardwalk overlooking the rapids.

(Photo by Stan Bradshaw)

Le Hardy Rapids Section

WHERE THE FISH STACK UP

Below the Estuary and about a half mile above Le Hardy Rapids, the river bottlenecks and builds up some speed before it goes into the rapids. There's some really ideal fishing to be had, and good bottom structure right above Le Hardy Rapids.

First you have to climb down the hill into the canyon, and, once you reach your destination, there's not a lot of room for casting on the bank. It takes a fairly good wader to wade out on to one of the little gravel bars in the area, to get in a good position to cast. So be careful here. If you're not confident in your wading skills, skip this one.

This fast water is also really good water for big nymphs, and large dry flies. You can cast upstream, mend your line, and the nymph will get down and bounce the bottom just right. And it's a fairly even flow in this section, though it is fast. It's just perfect nymph fishing.

This is heavy canyon water with "Salmon Fly" written all over it. All the larger stonefly nymphs will work in this section. I prefer the Brook's Stone in size 4 or my Giant Salmon Fly Nymph in size 4. From mid-July through early August, large Salmon Flies and Giant Western Golden Stones will hatch. When the hatch is on, I use my Salmon Fly dry fly in size 4 and my Golden Stone in size 6. Later in the season, after the Salmon Fly hatch is over, any large attractor fly like the Royal Wulff is a good bet. Presentation becomes more important than the pattern. When dry-fly fishing this fast canyon water, you need to get a drag-free float. This means you need to use short casts, reach casts, and mend your line, so practice your line control before you get here.

The Le Hardy Rapids themselves are quite dangerous, and the Park officials are not keen on people wading in them, so fishing is not allowed right at the rapids. It is a great place to

When fishing the Yellowstone, be mindful to follow the regulations. Some areas are closed for wildlife viewing, and others, like Le Hardy Rapids, for safety considerations.

view, and there's a high overlook at that point to see the rapids from. Right below the rapids is some really key water. The fish hold and stage here for extended periods to feed and rest before moving through. This is especially true as the fish move back upriver toward the lake later in the season.

This is a popular area, and you're likely to run into some crowding. Because you can't wade out in the center of this reach very easily, you are mostly confined to the bank or, at best, a few feet from shore. As a result, this area can get to feeling overpopulated pretty quickly.

Nonetheless, this stretch can be especially good during a hatch. The insects run large; you'll get big Salmon Flies, emerging caddisflies, and smaller stoneflies. You'll likely have everything at the same time. The trout in this section seem to orient a little more to the surface. They will come up for a dry fly or they'll take a nymph right under the surface. This is a good place to use a dry fly with a trailing nymph.

As these fish start working their way back toward Yellowstone Lake after spawning, they show up at the base of Le Hardy Rapids. The fish seem to stop there for a while, to rest and feed before they challenge the rapids, to go back up into the Estuary area. The good fishing extends down for about a half a mile, maybe a little more, until the river comes in close to the road again. Where it meets the road, the water gets pretty deep; it's tough to fish along the bank, and it's virtually impossible to fish the center of the river, so you have an area that's good holding water for fish, but not really very good for fishing.

Like most of the water from the lake to the Upper Falls of the Yellowstone, the river is most productive from around the opening, July 15, through August 15. After August 15, the water gets lower, most of the major hatches have ended, and many of the lake fish have passed through here and have moved up to the Estuary and the lake. But even in late summer the cutthroats will still rise to a well-presented dry fly. A good rule of thumb is to use large attractors—sizes 8 to 12—like the Royal Wulff, Goofus Bug, or a hopper pattern in heavy water. As you get into September and October, work the slower water for good hatches of Blue-Winged Olives with patterns like the Olive Parachute or Olive ComparaDun on size-16 hooks.

Buffalo Ford

LOTS OF TROUT AND LOTS OF PEOPLE

The river changes character below Le Hardy Rapids. About two miles, or a mile and a half below, it starts to widen out. It shallows, slows up slightly and the bottom becomes gravelly. At this point, it's easy to wade. There has been a picnic area at Buffalo Ford as long as I can remember. But just before the picnic area, the river meanders close to the road. There's an island there, and starting at the head of

Anglers array themselves along the productive and accessible area just across from the Cascade picnic area to fish the sweet spot above Buffalo Ford.

the island on the road side, the Park Service has set this area aside as a public viewing area with a special platform for the purpose of viewing cutthroat in their native habitat. There is no fishing or wading on this short inside section of the river.

Buffalo Ford is actually a shallow gravel bar which zigzags its way from just below the island up and across the river. As the name suggests, bison like to cross the river at this point. The water is shallow and fast as it moves through the ford, but it provides some of the best dry-fly fishing in the country. And it gets plenty of attention. It can get unbelievably crowded during the height of the season.

The prime fishing locations on Buffalo Ford are usually pretty consistent from one year to the next. I can remember some high-water years where you would park your car and cast while standing alongside the car, and catch fish on the grass. On the other hand, in 1987, we had an extremely low-water year. Some of the best fishing was right up against the

Bob Jacklin's dad, Robert Jacklin, lands a nice cutthroat trout at the famous Buffalo Ford. Note the other anglers spread out along the shallow gravel bar which offers some of the finest dry-fly fishing in the world.

banks in ankle deep water. Yet, in low water, you'll see people wade right through good holding water on their way to fish other water. The fish weren't spooked by the people. And that's what you have to remember when you're fishing the ford. You have to work the shallows unless there's an insect hatch on that brings them up.

Most of the time, however, the fish at Buffalo Ford respond to the hatches. When there's no hatch, the fish are going to move back to the holding areas and just stay there. When the hatch starts, they know before the fishermen. They'll move up to feeding places and feeding lanes, and that's where you'll get them. And a lot of times, that will be the shallow water.

When you come right off the picnic area, there is a little bowl that extends down along the bank just downstream of the parking area and there's always three or four fish in there. As you step off the bank, a small wooded island is directly facing you. A deep run goes right down along that island. Beyond the island, there is another, deeper run. If you circle around upstream of this small island, you can get above the point of the island and wade and fish toward the far shore. You'll find another deep run along that far shore. This one starts near the bank, cuts away from the bank, and comes right down the middle of the river.

On an average year you can wade this stretch. But you should be careful to wade around the channels and not in them, because the volume of the Yellowstone is deceptive. It's easy to wade because the bottom is pebbly and gravelly and footing is good—until you get to about chest deep. Once you get up near chest deep, you'll start to catch the volume and it can knock you down. So it's a little tricky. I've gotten wet several times in the Buffalo Ford area and had to swim my way out of some of those deep holes.

There are two ways to fish Buffalo Ford. You concentrate on the fish in the shallows or else you concentrate on the fish in the channels. The fish in the shallows will take nymphs and dry flies.

To reach the fish in the channels when they aren't rising you have to get your fly down to the bottom. The channel fish will hold on the bottom. So if you can get a nymph down to them, you might be able to entice them to strike. When those fish aren't rising, use a sinking line, short leader, and a size-8 Woolly Bugger with a black or peacock body and black marabou tail.

Generally, however, your best choice will be the shallow water, where the chance of seeing surface-feeding fish is much better. The fish concentrate in the shallows to feed.

The fish are always there around Buffalo Ford. Often you won't see them rise, you won't see them break, but there will always be a few fish nymphing. If you stalk them and spot them, you can take them.

Just below Buffalo Ford author Bob Jacklin instructs a fly fishing class.

Ray Bergman recounted in *Trout* that, in crossing a riffle while wading to a pool in the Catskill Mountains, he managed to stir up enough food that the fish started feeding, and he started catching fish. This phenomenon occurs quite often at Buffalo Ford. At the ford, if you stir up those riffles, those fish are going to come up and hold in your wake, feeding on the nymphs that you have dislodged.

The fish on Buffalo Ford see a lot of wading anglers. But you still may have to give them some time to acclimate to your presence. How long depends on how heavily the fish are feeding. In an area or time when the fish are feeding enthusiastically and there are lots of insects around, you can walk through a pool, turn around and catch a fish. When they're not feeding as heavily, and there are not as many insects on the water, you might stir that area up and put them off their feed for a few minutes. In that case, ignore those fish for a while so they can get used to you. Usually, there will be some other fish you can cast to.

Sulphur Caldron

ROTTEN EGGS AND TRICKY FISH

Below Buffalo Ford, the river makes a turn to the left and heads pretty much due west, toward the road again. And down a short path, there's a couple of small islands and a larger island. The fishing in this stretch can be excellent; as a young guide, I spent a lot of my time along those islands. I worked for over ten years with the Fenwick Fly Fishing Schools, and during the summer season, we would take the Fenwick class to the Buffalo Ford picnic area to fish every Wednesday. I would take three or four students with me to the islands just below the ford for the morning or afternoon session. It is a great place to learn about rising trout, entomology, fly selection, and aquatic life in general. And it's a great place to catch fish—the perfect introduction to fly fishing.

Upstream from the Sulphur Caldron lies one of the most scenic areas of the river.

There are some places that are deep and hard to wade, but if you can get out to one of the islands, especially the large island, you can really have a whole day of fishing just around that one island without the pressure of the crowds that you get around Buffalo Ford.

As you get into the Sulphur Caldron area, you're going to know it pretty quickly simply by the smell. It smells like rotten eggs. After a while you get so use to it that it's almost pleasing. Smell aside, the fishing is really good. This stretch always holds at least a few good size trout.

The turn-off right at the Sulphur Caldron offers a chance to look down at some big fish. There's a point of trees and an outcropping at the turn-off. If you walk out after 1:00 p.m. and put on your polaroid sunglasses, you can look straight down into a small eddy below a whirlpool at what appear to be huge fish. Actually, they average about a pound and a half to 2 pounds, but they

From the outcropping above Sulphur Caldron, which bubbles up just west of the river, you can see the deep eddy where large trout can sometimes be observed sipping small dry flies (in the center foreground of the photo above). About fifty yards below the eddy, the river is closed to fishing as it enters Hayden Valley. Watch for the closed sign as you fish downstream.

look like they're 4 to 5 pounds from the road, and anybody that wasn't used to the fishing there would swear that they were 5-pounders. You can see these big fish sipping on small midges and insects in that little eddy. To get down to the water from the parking area, go down the hill to the left of the slide, through the trees. Remember you have about one hundred yards of open water to fish before the river enters Hayden Valley and is closed to fishing.

The eddy itself is really tough to fish. It is surrounded by a variety of currents which make a presentation difficult. To show you how tough it can be, I had the pleasure of spending the whole day with Lee and Joan Wulff many years ago on that particular spot. Lee fished for over an hour, changing to smaller flies and then cutting his fly smaller and smaller with a pair of scissors, until finally he was pretty much fishing a size-24 pupa before he started taking fish. It is a tough spot, even for someone of his skills.

You have tremendous problems with drag at this eddy. One approach is to fish a longer rod—13 feet isn't too long—just for the purpose of lifting the tip high enough to get most of the line off the water. The drag is a big enough problem, but when you add in the wind which whistles through the canyon here, getting a good drift in the eddy can be almost impossible. The long rod, or an extra long tippet, will help give you a little bit of natural float before the drag catches.

Aside from tough currents, wind can be a serious challenge around Sulphur Caldron. It can come at you from almost any direction. If I was given a choice, I would prefer to have it either blowing from my left to right or coming into my face. I think I can handle it better that way. You can cast into it and you have more control than you do when it's coming from the side, or even when it's coming over the back.

If the wind is strong and blowing straight downstream, you can use it to your advantage by casting upriver well above your target. The wind will drop your fly and leader downstream of your line and float the fly into the feeding fish ahead of the line. If the wind is blowing upriver, use a quartering-upstream approach and lengthen your tippet.

At Sulphur Caldron you have heat coming into the river. That temperature doesn't immediately dissipate on entering the river, so you have a temperature line. The fish stack up on temperature lines like this one; they'll be holding in the cool water, then they'll move toward the warmer water and take an insect, and then move out again. Find a thermal and you'll find fish.

With polaroids, you can often pick out one fish and look ten feet below, see another fish and then another fish, right

Hayden Valley, where the Yellowstone River meanders across a former lakebed, is a mating area for Park bison and a great place to view wildlife all season long.

(Photo by Stan Bradshaw)

on down the river. When you find this concentration, start with the bottom fish and work your way up.

In fact, a good rule for all waters, even when you can't see the fish, is to start fishing the shallow water near shore first. This water, often only four to six inches deep, may seem too shallow to hold fish, but don't wade until you have fished it. Then, and only then, move on to the deeper and "better looking" water. I have caught many good-sized—and even trophy-sized—fish by covering the close, shallow water first.

The Hayden Valley

CLOSED FOR WILDLIFE

Just below the Sulphur Caldron, the Yellowstone River widens out, slows up a little bit, and speads out into a

The Yellowstone River through Hayden Valley, seen above with snow on the ground, has lots of weed beds that provide an ideal nursery for young cutthroat trout. Closed to fishing, it is well posted.

(Photo by Stan Bradshaw)

beautiful valley. This is Hayden Valley. There's no fishing in Hayden Valley, all the way from the Sulphur Caldron to the confluence with Alum Creek. This area is set aside for viewing wildlife. Bald eagles, osprey, all sorts of ducks, birds, geese. And don't forget the grizzly bears, moose, bison, and elk. About three miles long by road, it's just a wonderful place for viewing wildlife. So even though you can't fish, it's a great place to take a breather and enjoy some of the other attractions in the park.

Alum Creek to Chittenden Bridge

From the confluence of Alum Creek to where the river rejoins the road, the river is deep, flat, wide, and lined with weed beds. The bottom is silty and home to one of the great western mayflies, the Western Green Drake. Around

These anglers are fishing the Green Drake hatch below the confluence of Alum Creek. Alum Creek itself is closed to fishing.

(Photo by Sharyn Jacklin)

August 10 or so, these large bright yellow-green mayflies with dun wings start to emerge. From mid-morning to early afternoon, the emergence of the Green Drake will trigger a feeding frenzy. The best fly for this hatch is the Western Green Drake Wulff, in about size 12. It is also good to carry some size-6 and size-8 hoppers this time of the year on this stretch, just in case.

Another good non-hatch tactic for this section is to use a small—about size 8—black or olive Woolly Bugger. Work it along and over the thick weed beds.

Chittenden Bridge

BANK FEEDERS ON THE BRINK

This section of the river isn't fished much, because it's quite wide and very deep. Spin fishing will work early in the

Chittenden Bridge above the Upper Falls of the Yellowstone River marks the beginning of an area closed to fishing that extends downstream to below the Lower Falls. Looking upriver toward Chittenden Bridge, the vantage point in the photo above offers a lovely view of the 109-foot Upper Falls and part of the closed area above and below it.

season, but you won't see many fly fishermen here. There are trout to be found in this stretch, however. Specifically, you'll find bank-sipping fish. You can take them with a fly rod and you can have really good fishing, but you have to change your tactics. Here, you have to spot the individual fish and stalk them.

Where the river comes near the road, cross the bridge and park and fish up the far side, carefully, along the bank. Try to spot bank sippers and approach them from below, casting straight upstream along the bank and along the many weed beds. This is about the only way you can effectively fish this stretch. Use a hopper or some other terrestrial.

If you decide to fish this stretch, time your fishing to the hatches. If the insects aren't there, this can be a really lonely place to fish because the trout are way out and you can't reach them. Even a real long distance caster cannot reach them.

The only time you'll be able to reach those fish in the middle is when the water is low and you can wade a little bit to where the large Green Drakes hatch out in early August. Then it becomes a little more worthwhile working this reach of the river.

One positive aspect of fishing here is that you probably won't feel crowded by other anglers. There's a lot of bank and you can just spread out and work the edges and wade out a little ways in some sections.

One caution about fishing near Chittenden Bridge—you don't want to get too close to the bridge. Upper Yellowstone Falls are just below it. It's best to stay well upstream and don't try to do too much fancy wading. In fact, I recommend that you not wade this stretch. If you lose your footing anywhere near that bridge, it could be the last mistake you ever make. Think of it this way: the fishing is just as good upstream of the bridge as it is down. Fly fishing isn't supposed to be a death sport.

The Grand Canyon

GREAT FISHING IN A GRAND SETTING

Directly below Chittenden Bridge, you have Upper Yellowstone Falls. Shortly below that, you have the spectacular Lower Falls. The water from the Upper Falls down to the Lower Falls is closed to fishing. Below the Lower Falls is the Grand Canyon of the Yellowstone. There are only a few trails that go down to the river in the canyon. One of the more notable is the Seven Mile Hole Trail. Seven Mile starts just outside Canyon Village and goes seven miles down and feels like about twenty miles back up. It's about a fifteen-hundred-foot descent.

It's a real pleasure to be down there. The fish are not any larger than they are up above. They're the same wild, beautiful cutthroat as you see upstream—perfect 15-, 16-, 17-inch fish, but it's a different kind of fishing. It's canyon water. You're not mobile down there. You can only wade out a short distance; it's deep water and you're limited to where you can go. You're primarily fishing big pools, for good-sized trout. One added feature is that while you'll still find mostly cutthroats in the canyon stretch you also may see some other species. Because you're below the falls, the fish can come up from the lower Yellowstone River, and you will occasionally see some rainbow and brown trout mixed in with the cutthroat.

This is a good place to use big nymphs or sculpin patterns. The sculpin population starts to pick up down there. Streamer and nymph techniques become a little bit more valuable in this heavy water. Remember, this is big, fast water and the trout that live here are conditioned to respond more quickly to available food.

Nonetheless, it is still excellent dry-fly water. This is good Salmon Fly water, too, so be prepared to fish big dry flies. Even when the Salmon Flies are gone, it's still great big-

The 1,000-foot precipice, 308-foot turbulent fall, and steep canyon walls of the Lower Falls of the Yellowstone illustrate the necessity of closing the area to fishing. The canyon and falls are visible from overlooks along the canyon rims.

(Photo by Stan Bradshaw)

Looking downstream from Inspiration Point, you can see the Grand Canyon of the Yellowstone. The only way to reach the river in this section is from the west rim via the Seven Mile Hole Trail. The hike is seven miles down into the canyon, but it will feel like twenty miles back up.

(Photo by Stan Bradshaw)

dry-fly water. Take a selection of large-sized Royal Wulffs, Hair Wing Variants, and Goofus Bugs, or any stonefly or hopper patterns. Anything large and those trout will come up even in the deepest water.

Remember, in canyon water like this many fish will feed on the bank, because that is where most of the food is. Fish upstream and cover the pockets, drop-offs, and runs along the banks with dry flies. Fish wet flies down and across and start your retrieve as the fly swings toward shore. Fish nymphs right along the edge, either with a short line or an indicator. Stonefly nymphs will migrate to the bank before emerging, so the trout will be looking for them there.

Browns and Rainbows of the Black Canyon

The Black Canyon section of the Yellowstone, roughly twenty miles of water, is largely inaccessible. There are a couple of good access points at the upper end—one at Tower Fall and one at Tower Junction, which goes right up along the river. The trail at Tower Fall drops down to lower Tower Creek and the main Yellowstone River just at the bottom of the Grand Canyon of the Yellowstone. This area has always been one of my favorite to fish and guide. It's a nice hike down a good trail, with lots of nice cutthroats in the main river as well as a mix of cutthroat and brook trout in Tower Creek.

You have a really varied river here. There are some deep holes, but there are also some well-defined runs and riffles. Tower Creek can be good early in the season. One additional plus for this section is that the fishing in the Yellowstone below the Lower Falls and in Tower Creek opens with the general season, on the Saturday before Memorial Day. On many occasions I have had good fishing on lower Tower Creek when the main river was too high and off-color.

The Black Canyon of the Yellowstone, photographed looking downstream from the Tower Creek area, is another difficult-to-access area of the river. Two trails that go into the mid-canyon stretch are Blacktail Creek Trail and Hellroaring Creek Trail.

There are two other access points or trail heads to the Black Canyon—the Hell Roaring Creek Trail and the Blacktail Creek Trail. A word of caution—these trails are considered "back country." They are steep and rugged, and you should be in good shape if you decide to take them.

There are some really deep holes that will reward the nymph fishermen, and some shallow riffles along the banks for those bank sippers, and there's a lot of wind and sagebrush in this reach, so you'll see plenty of hoppers. This is excellent hopper water, especially later in the summer.

The species composition begins to show more diversity in this reach. You will see more browns and rainbows than upstream. These species, particularly, like to feed on the banks where the hoppers are. But the cutthroats, too, will move in along the banks, especially on a deep section right along the ledges or walls where the canyon goes straight. Just fishing straight upstream with a hopper will bring some of these fish up in mid-August when there is seemingly nothing else going on. During a exceptionally warm year, you may see hoppers active in this stretch even through September.

Another good tactic for this stretch is to skate a stonefly pattern. Twitch a big stonefly across the surface. This will often bring up the fish better than the same pattern fished dead-drift. You're exciting the fish's predatory instinct. Fish it the way you would a streamer, only keep it on top. As with the hoppers, you can use this tactic effectively late into the summer, long past when you would normally assume that stoneflies are no longer active on the surface. That is because Golden Stones will hatch there all through August, much as they will on the lower Gallatin and some of the other rivers that have a lot of freestone and canyon-type water. Black Canyon's resident trout are always aware that there are stoneflies of some sort around.

As the river flows north out of the Park toward Gardiner, there is some excellent fishing where the Gardner River enters the Yellowstone just upstream of the town of Gardiner.

The early season on Yellowstone Lake offers an excellent opportunity for beginning anglers to catch native cutthroat trout that congregate near shore as the water warms and offers an abundance of food after a long, hard winter.

CHAPTER 2

Seasons of the River

EARLY SEASON
JUNE 15 TO JULY 15

In my book, the early season on the Yellowstone drainage starts with the opening of Yellowstone Lake on June 15. The river from below the Lower Falls to the Park boundary opens with the general season, but high water makes fishing there before June 15 impractical in most years.

Historically, Yellowstone Lake opened on June 15, but in the late 1990s the Park enacted an earlier opening for a couple of years, hoping to encourage anglers to catch the predatory lake trout that compete with the native cutthroats. Instead, fishers were catching thousands more cutthroats. To preserve the cutthroats, the Park set the opening day back to the traditional June 15 date and expanded its catch-and-release regulation to include the cutthroat trout in Yellowstone Lake.

Lake trout populations were, I believe, illegally planted in the lake sometime before 1970. Between 1994, when they were first discovered in Yellowstone Lake, and 2000 the National Park Service had removed 237,000 lake trout from the lake. Despite removal efforts, by 2000 cutthroat numbers had dropped to their lowest level in about twenty-five years, according to Park officials.

Lake trout prefer cold, deep water, making them difficult to catch. The one exception to this deep water behavior is in the spring when lake trout move toward shore at ice-out to feed in the warmer, shallower waters. If you catch a lake trout, you have to keep it. If you want to try your hand at this, work the shore around the West Thumb of the lake in early June.

Most of the people who fish Yellowstone Lake use lures and jigs because, early in the season, the fish are down deep even though they're pretty close to shore. Early-season anglers will catch a lot of fish on ¼-ounce or ⅜-ounce lures. For fly fishing, you need a full-sinking line with a weighted Woolly Bugger or other streamer. Fish the streamer as deep as you can. It is not exactly classic, elegant fly fishing, but it can work really well.

There is an occurrence on the lake that can offer an alternative to deep-running flies early in the season. Wind will drive big waves into shore, stirring up the shallow bottom and creating a mud line. Fish like to feed on those mud lines because food, driven into shore by waves and wind, concentrates along that line. I've been on Yellowstone Lake in the morning before the wind come up and had poor fishing. Once the wind comes up for about an hour, I start catching more fish as the fish move in from the deeper water. It's just like a river, the trout have their holding water and their feeding water. When the wind is up, that mud line is their feeding water.

The mud line also eliminates the need for long casts into deep water. As a matter of fact, it's counterproductive to cast out into that barren water and bring the fly back. It's best to wade out, get in at around knee-deep water and cast parallel to that mud and bring the fly right along the edge of it. Try to keep your fly just on the clear edge. Think of it as Rocky Mountain surf fishing.

These fish are cruisers, so you can hit a pocket, you can catch two or three fish and then you'll have a few dead moments. If you fish the same area and stay with it, you've got a chance of getting some fish coming your way. A black Woolly Bugger with maybe a little of that Krystal Flash or Crystal Hair, in about a size 8, is a good fly for fishing these mud lines. These fish won't take it aggressively like a brown or rainbow would in say, 55-degree water. Slow your retrieve a little bit. If that doesn't work, then vary your retrieve; try fast, try slow, try intermediate retrieves.

Another effective technique would be to fish a weighted size-10 nymph or traditional wet fly. Cast it on that mud line and let it sink and do nothing else. Watch the line tip, and if you see it twitch, set the hook. This can be a deadly method for working the mud. If you have trouble seeing the line tip, you can use a strike indicator.

The Yellowstone River below Upper and Lower Yellowstone Falls opens on the Saturday before Memorial Day. Above the falls, it opens on July 15.

Below the falls the river has a lot of stonefly nymph activity. The Salmon Fly hatch is in this section of the river in early July, still a little lower down river from the falls. But the big *Pteronarcys* nymphs will be really active, so big, black weighted nymphs are a good choice. Fish them on a floating line, with maybe a non-lead split shot or two because the river will be high and rolling this time of year. Good

The quarter mile or so of Tower Creek between 132-foot Tower Fall and the Yellowstone River is a good place to fish in early July. It opens with the general season that usually falls on the Saturday before Memorial Day, but its flow will run too high for angling for the first several weeks.

pattern choices include the Jacklin Giant Salmon Fly Nymph, Brook's Stone, Bitch Creek, Black Girdle Bug, Black Woolly Worm, Woolly Bugger, and Natural Drift Stonefly Nymph in sizes 4 to 8. The key words here are *big* and *black*. Stonefly nymphs move toward the bank where they will eventually crawl out to hatch , so you don't need to fish beyond the edges during high water. Keep a short line and fish close to the bank.

There is one other tactic that can help offset the effect of high flows this time of the year. Find slow back-water areas in the canyon stretch, and work weighted flies through these areas. The fish will seek shelter from the fast current in the slack water.

If the main river feels a little too big and fast, consider Tower Creek. Tower Creek is a great little stream to fish. It only runs for about a quarter of a mile from Tower Fall before it dumps into the Yellowstone River. Lower Tower Creek is a great place for beginning fly fishers. The stream is short and swift, with lots of pocket water. In June and early July, cutthroats stack up in Tower Creek and will attack whatever fly you put before them. Later in the summer, after most of the cutthroats have moved back into the river, you'll still find some good fishing for decent-sized brook trout. And since you're down there, it might be worth trying the Yellowstone around the mouth of Tower Creek. It can be good all season long.

MID-SEASON
JULY 15 TO AUGUST 20

Think of the mid-season as starting with the traditional opening day on the upper river of July 15 and running until

The hatch of the giant Salmon Fly progresses upstream from the lower Yellowstone in Montana beginning in June. You can always fish Salmon Fly imitations somewhere on the upper river by opening day, July 15.

August 20. By July 15, the Salmon Fly hatches should be in full swing and the classic mayfly and caddis hatches are beginning. You can choose the water you want to fish by deciding what insect you want to fish.

If you want to fish the Salmon Fly, find some heavy water. The stretch right above Le Hardy Rapids is great Salmon Fly water.

If you want to fish mayflies, caddis, or small stoneflies, the riffle section above and below Buffalo Ford is a good place to start.

The Grannom caddisfly, *Brachycentrus* sp., will show up just about anywhere there is fast water. Look for the little four-sided cases in the river bed. The emerging insect will have a green body and mottled varied-colored wing. Match it with a size-14 fly. Good patterns include LaFontaine's

This happy angler caught a trophy cutthroat on a Blue-Winged Olive dry fly just below the Sulphur Caldron in August. The Black Spotted Cutthroat rises slowly and deliberately and gives the fisherman the full visual effect of the strike.

Emergent Sparkle Pupa and the EZ2C Caddis and the Fluttering Gray Caddis, also called the Reverse-Wing Caddis.

If you want to try the Gray Drake, *Siphlonurus occidentalis,* go up to the Estuary just below the lake. The Gray Drake hatch doesn't last all that long—you probably have a fifteen-day window when you can focus on the hatch. But you can have some exceptional fishing while the Gray Drakes are hatching. I especially enjoy the Gray Drake spinner fall in the evenings.

In addition to hatches, water conditions may affect your opening-day decisions about where to fish. If you run into high water—with water running up to or over the top of the banks—consider fishing right below the Buffalo Ford area. There is some slower water there, and the fish will cruise in and feed right on the grassy banks. Another good high-water area would be quite a bit above Le Hardy Rapids where the Estuary starts to speed up just above the canyon into the Le Hardy Rapids. This section is quite wide and looks more like a lake than a river.

In low-water years, your options for where you can find good fishing are much broader. One of my low-water favorites is the cluster islands below Buffalo Ford. If you can get to them, you will likely find good fish rising all the way around the islands.

The mid-season will offer some dry-fly fishing just about anywhere along the upper Yellowstone above the falls. Below the falls, to the park boundary near Gardiner, the Salmon Fly hatch will be in full swing somewhere. The hatch will start on the lower Yellowstone near Livingston and progress up the river past the Gardiner area, into the Park, and all the way to the Lower Falls. This provides great fishing with large Salmon Fly imitations. The hatch is usually in the lower river around Black Canyon and Tower Junction by mid-July.

LATE SEASON
AUGUST 20 THROUGH OCTOBER

One mayfly that signals the change from mid-season to late season is the Small Western Red Quill, *Rhithrogena undulata*. It's usually coming off by the July 15 opening and can actively hatch for up to a month. You'll find it all over the river—on the riffles and on the rapids—and the fish come readily to it. And then, in early to mid-August, it starts to peter out and the fishing gets a little bit harder. The one dry fly that seems to work great during the Red Quill hatch is the Light Cahill, although I have always thought that the

Hendrickson was a better match. Day in and day out, the old standard Adams and the Parachute Adams are two flies you can count on. For the evening spinner fall, I like the Rusty Para-Spin, with a thin rusty dubbing, a short post, and an oversized grizzly hackle tied parachute style, in sizes 14 and 16.

In fact, many of the major hatches start to fade in early to mid-August. The fish start to key on the spinner falls in the evening, so during the day, they're probably not feeding as heavily on the duns. Also, at this time of the year, we start to lose the fish in the river as they begin to slowly move back toward the lake.

But there are still fish to be found, and while fishing the hatches won't be as productive anymore during the middle of the day, there are still some great opportunities this time of the year. As the hatches fade, the terrestrials are just coming into their own.

The cutthroats are a dry-fly angler's delight. They are conditioned to rise, so they'll take a small ant, a flying ant, a beetle—anything floating on the surface that looks like it's food. They'll also take a big hopper. But you have to go one way or the other. You either have to go with a size-8 hopper or you have to go with a size-16 or a size-18 terrestrial. Too many people are still using the size 12s and 14s, and those won't be as productive for terrestrials.

Between the small insects and the large, fishing the smaller ones tends to be more productive. You can locate a fish and might entice it on the big hopper but you're more apt to get them on an ant or a smaller beetle. If you don't locate a surface-feeding fish, you want to fish the center of the river or the center of a deep pool, with a big fly. In the deep water, you need to make it worth the trout's trouble to come all the way up and take that fly. The big bite of food is the attraction to pull it to the top.

Heavy canyon water in the Tower area yielded this nice cutthroat to a grasshopper pattern.

(Photo by Collin Brown)

Some good, reliable terrestrial patterns include a Fur Ant with a black hackle in the center, a Crowe Beetle with a peacock body, Jacklin's Hopper, or Dave's Hopper. One of my favorite patterns is my looped-wing poly ant pattern, which is a black and cinnamon color with a flying loop wing. It has been an excellent producer on the Yellowstone. I developed the Looped-Wing Flying Ant to match the flying ant hatch. For years, we used a small Royal Wulff as an indicator for a regular ant below it, but I was never really satisfied with that combination. So, I came up with the poly ant. It is easy to tie, floats well, and is really visible. I clip the bottom of the hackle flat so the ant lies flat in the surface film.

Even during the middle of the day, you can pull fish up. You get species of stoneflies that are not important anywhere else in the world. One, for example, is the Giant Western Golden Stone, a midsummer insect. It's a big insect, requiring an imitation in a size-4 to size-6 fly. It likely won't appear in huge numbers, but it comes off about the time other insects are slowing down, so the fish are always aware of them. Good skating technique will bring fish up on the Yellowstone River. A good pattern to skate is the Jacklin's Golden Stone. Once the hatches start to decline, if the fish see something that's moving, looks alive on the surface, they'll investigate.

Another mid- to late-season hatch is the lake fly, or Speckled Spinner (*Callibaetis ferrugineus*), starting about August 1 and continuing through the rest of the summer. You'll see this one in the Estuary. A good imitation for the *Callibaetis* is a large (size 14), predominantly gray pattern such as a an Adams or an Adams Parachute. I like a Gray Wulff if the fish are not too fussy. When they get a little more particular, I'll use a *Callibaetis* Para-Spin, which doubles as a spinner or a dun.

In the Buffalo Ford area, use a spinner-type pattern in the evening, maybe a spent-wing Adams or a Rusty Para-Spin for the Red Quill spinner.

Caddisflies become important this time of the year. I've seen days when I pulled up on the river about four o'clock in the afternoon in late July or early August, and the whole surface would look like it was boiling because trout would be slashing and chasing emerging caddis all over the place. When the caddis are emerging, it can be difficult to catch fish consistently. If you stick to a floating fly, you may get a few strikes, but you're actually fishing with something other than what the fish are feeding on. If you fish downstream and swing an emerger or fish an emerger on the rise, the trout are sometime so aggressive that they'll take your fly and leave you with a great strike, no fly, and, of course, no fish. One of the best methods to use during a heavy caddis emergence is to fish the emerger just under the surface in a dead-drift. When you see a boil where you think your fly is, strike. Two great patterns for this are LaFontaine's Emergent Sparkle Pupa and the Soft Hackle in sizes 14 and 16.

The Yellowstone is a premier midge river, and the emergence of midges in this late season can drive a fisherman crazy. The flies are tiny, and a lot of anglers just don't make the match. One tactic is to walk slowly along the bank and try to find bank-feeders and the odd fish that might be feeding when no other fish is feeding and very little is on the water. That fish is likely to be eating midges and you need to fish small flies to it. A Griffith's Gnat, in sizes 18 and 20, is a good general midge pattern for the Yellowstone.

The Yellowstone gets a good Trico fall in the late season. About ten o'clock in the morning, the spinners are on the water and the fish will come to them. The Trico Para-Spin has proven to be a successful imitation over the years. The Trico Para-Spin is a small parachute-style Trico that is easy to see on the water. It has a black body, a forked tail, and an oversized grizzly hackle to imitate the spent wings. The fish like it. Use this in sizes 18 and 20.

As the season moves into late August, early September, the fishing will pick up when we get cloud cover. The Blue-Winged Olive, *Baetis tricaudatus*, comes into its own about 3:30 in the afternoon. As the season progresses, the Blue-Winged Olive becomes the key for late-season fishing on the Yellowstone River. *Baetis* nymphs, emergers, dry flies, and drowned spinner imitations will be an important part of your late-season pattern collection.

You can get into some good Blue-Winged Olive hatches as late as the end of September on the Yellowstone, but by then fish have started to migrate back into the lake, so there aren't nearly as many fish in the river. You have to pick your water carefully. The fishing in the Buffalo Ford area is pretty well over, but below the ford there are some areas around the Sulphur Caldron that will hold fish and you'll find some in the Estuary. But, on balance, fishing will get tough by late September above the falls. One strategy would be to go below the falls. You stand a fair chance of finding more fish around the Black Canyon area in late September.

A natural adult Salmon Fly poses with a Jacklin's Giant Salmon Fly.

CHAPTER 3

Dry Flies

If I had to carry just one box of dry flies on the upper Yellowstone, it would be a pretty big box. I would start with a good supply of Adams, size 12 and size 14, and the Adams Parachute in sizes 14 and 16. For the evening, hatches I would include the standard Quill Gordon for the Red Quill in size 16. I would want the Rusty Para-Spin and the Orange Double Wing and Orange EZ2C. No dry-fly selection would be complete without a good supply of stonefly patterns. For the stoneflies, I would want the Jacklin's Salmon Fly in a size 4, the Flex-Stone, the Golden Stonefly in sizes 6 and 8, and some Little Yellow Stones in size 10. For mid-season, I would want a good selection of Green Drakes in sizes 12 and 14 and Gray Wulffs in size 14. As we get into the late season, terrestrials play an important part, so I add grasshopper patterns in sizes 8 and 10, a couple of beetles and ants, and the *Callibaetis* Para-Spin for the Estuary. I also would include a selection of Royal Wulffs in sizes 10 through 14, a few Trico imitations, Griffith's Gnats in sizes 18 and 20, and a good selection of Blue-Winged Olives in standard, ComparaDun, and parachute dressings. Again, it would take a big box, but then, the upper Yellowstone is a big dry-fly river, and if you want to be prepared for it, this is what you'll need, at a minimum.

Parachute Patterns

Anyone coming to fish the upper Yellowstone would do well to come loaded with a wide array of parachute-style fly patterns. Day in and day out, low-profile dry flies are extremely effective on the upper Yellowstone. I am most partial toward parachute-style dry flies. No-hackle patterns are great—they really fool a lot of fish—but I don't think they are as durable as the parachute. Also, the parachute tie floats a little easier and it's easier to see .

Another advantage of the parachute-style patterns is that they are effective for both the dun and spinner stages of the mayfly hatches. I have found a black-bodied parachute in size 18 or size 20 to be extremely effective on the Trico hatches. The Tricos key on that black body. I tie my Para-Spin with a sparse black body, a short post, a grizzly parachute hackle, and a forked tail. It's difficult to see a regular spinner pattern, especially for the Trico, but you can see the Para-Spin. And the fish aren't put off by the post. Fish this pattern during the Trico hatch just below the Estuary or at Buffalo Ford.

Parachutes are great for more than just the small flies, however. While most of my parachutes are in the range of sizes 14 to 16, I will tie as large as a size 10 or 12 for the Brown Drake and Green Drake hatches. That's the great thing about the parachute styles. You can tie them to match just about any fly—and any size fly— you want, from tiny mayflies to caddisflies to hoppers.

Yellowstone Park is grizzly bear country. Take care that you don't become an "attractor" yourself! Bears frequent trails, streams, and lakeshores and, like you, are anglers. Heed Park warnings about bears, carry bear spray, make noise to make your presence known, and, should you encounter a bear, give it plenty of room, detour if possible, or wait for the bear to move on.

(Photo by Collin Brown)

If there is a drawback to parachute patterns, it is on rough water. They don't handle the chop and slosh of riffles as well as standard hackle dry flies. So, if you fish the rougher water on the upper Yellowstone, you may want to complement your parachute patterns with similar imitations in the standard dressings.

Attractors

My favorite attractor on the upper Yellowstone is the Royal Wulff. The Wulff is easy to see and it's been a constant producer over the years, especially for late-season fishing. It is at its best on sunny days. One August day many years ago during one of the Federation of Fly Fishers Conclaves I found myself at Sulphur Caldron with my dad and Joan and Lee Wulff. The day started slow—no surface activity and no insects on the water. Right after lunch, Joan tied on a size-10 Royal Wulff. The combination of a bright sunny day, a good drift, a little luck, and the Royal Wulff turned the tide. Joan started catching fish in mid-river over deep water. The great big Royal Wulff was like a magnet for those big cutthroats. We all followed Joan's lead, switched flies, and caught fish all afternoon. I have taken that approach many times since then with similar success.

Gary LaFontaine's Double Wing series of down-wing flies, both highly bouyant and visible, are designed to match the various light conditions. When used intelligently, they can increase your catches on attractor dry flies. The theory behind them is simple. Use a warm color fly, such as the Orange Double Wing, in the evening when the sun is low and the light is reddish orange. Use a cooler color fly, such as the Lime Double Wing, during midday when the sun is high. Other patterns in the series, such as the Gray Double Wing, Royal Double Wing, the Pink Lady Double Wing, the Yellow Double Wing, and the White Double Wing, round out the selection. Carry these in sizes 8 through 16.

On a gray day, I'm more inclined to fish something in an olive, maybe leaning toward the *Baetis*-type fly. In fact, on most overcast days, I tend to lean toward matching the hatch, and I'm less inclined to use an attractor.

Matching the Hatch

Of all the mayfly hatches on the Yellowstone River, the Little Red Quill is probably the toughest to match. I've had times trying to match that hatch when I tried everything from an olive to a gray, and still got clobbered. It's possible to run into that problem with almost any insect species on the river at one time or another.

But you can apply a basic hatching-matching approach that will serve you well in most situations. It's a three step approach that looks at size, silhouette, and color. While the perfect situation is to have a combination of all three of these things, if you have to prioritize, then first try to match size, then silhouette, and third, color.

As to size, try to match the insect's size as closely as you can. Even if you do match the size, your fly is likely to look larger than the actual insect on the water, but that probably is to your advantage. Being opportunistic, trout will often pick out your fly over the many naturals on the water because it looks larger—more food for the effort expended.

Silhouette, as seen from below, is important, because that is how the trout sees it. How many tails does it have? Is the body long or short? Is the wing spent or upright? Will a standard hackle help or hinder the perception of the fly? What about a parachute or no-hackle? These are variables that you can control, and attention to the details of silhouette can turn a slow day into a busy day on the water.

I believe that trout can see and distinguish color and shades of color. I first try to match the body color of the insect, then the color of the wing. For example, when I match the dun, I try to use a medium blue dun for the hackle to match a slate or gray wing. On matching the spinner, I will often use a grizzly hackle because it reflects light much like the clear spent wing of the natural insect.

One key to matching any hatch is to recognize when the fish are truly taking dry flies, and when they're only taking emergers. There may be nothing more frustrating than casting to a bunch of apparently surface-feeding fish who never hit your perfectly matched dry fly. When that happens, it's time to look at how the fish are really feeding.

One simple test is to look at what's actually on the surface. If you look at the surface and there are lots of dries on the water, then they're probably taking the dries, and you need to tinker with the size-color-profile scheme. But, if you only see a few dries, and yet they're rising all over the place, they're likely taking the emergers.

With a little practice, you can quickly tell whether the trout are feeding on the dry fly or sipping the emergers just by watching them feed. On the larger fish you can see the trout's head and mouth break the surface when they take dries off the top of the water. If you just see fish backs or dorsal fins breaking the surface, they are feeding on the emerging nymphs. If all you see are tails, then the trout are feeding on the bottom. Splashy rises may indicate one of two possibilities—small fish or fish rising to caddis. Caddisflies emerge vigorously and induce the fish to rise aggressively. You'll usually be able to distinguish the splashy rise of a big fish from that of a little fish.

It is very common to see fish taking emergers during caddisfly hatches. You will often see anglers fishing an Elk Hair Caddis during caddis hatches and not moving fish. This usually happens when the fish are focused on caddis emergers. Most of the time, trout will feed on caddisflies beneath the surface. The free-swimming caddis worm and the cased caddis make up a good part of the trout's diet on the bottom of the stream. During times of heavy caddis emergence, the trout will chase the fast-emerging caddis to the surface and beyond. These splashy rises may fool us into thinking the fish are taking flies on the surface when they actually are feeding just below the surface. As a practical matter, I think the Elk Hair Caddis is most effective as a small stonefly imitation. While the Elk Hair Caddis will take some fish during the emergence, it is simply in the wrong place to attract most of the fish feeding on emergers. Use an emerger just under the surface, or swing a wet fly or soft-hackled fly through the caddis-feeding fish, and hold on.

The Elk Hair Caddis is at its best on the upper Yellowstone as an imitation for the small yellow and olive stoneflies. When you see these flies fluttering around it's a good indication that the trout know they're available, and a Yellow Elk Hair Caddis in a size 14 or size 16 is an effective imitation.

One effective tactic on the Yellowstone is to twitch your dry flies, especially on a windy day. This tactic will work not just with caddis patterns, terrestrial patterns, or stonefly patterns, but with mayfly patterns as well. Yellowstone fish tend to be cruisers. They'll move to the natural or the artificial on the surface, as opposed to waiting for the fly to come to them. The secret is to make it twitch upstream. Natural insects try to move upstream, so you don't want it dragging downstream.

One of the most annoying things for dry-fly anglers new to cutthroat fishing is their slow take of the dry fly. Most people new to cutthroat fishing will tend to strike too quickly. When you see the take, pause a beat before lifting your rod tip to set the hook.

Cutthroats stack up to feed below Le Hardy Rapids, where the even flow of the riffle offers good nymph fishing.

Chapter 4

Nymphs

lthough the Yellowstone River in the Park is the classic dry-fly river, occasionally you do need nymphs.

Naturally, the best time is for nymphs is when there's no surface activity. It's still early in the season or early in the morning, and the trout have not surfaced yet. They're on the bottom, they're occasionally picking up something down there, and you have to get your fly down to them. That means nymph fishing.

If you decide to fish nymphs, a good rule of thumb is to fish the deep sections because the trout tend to use those areas as holding waters when there are no insect hatches. Work the channels that run 3½ to 4 feet deep.

The most effective approach is to use a floating line with an indicator. I use a 12- to 13-foot leader. I prefer to use a nymph on which the weight was incorporated into the body when it was tied, but if your nymphs aren't weighted, add some non-lead split shot on the leader above the fly. Another effective way to weight your fly is to use a bead-head fly. It not only adds weight, but it adds some shine to the head of the fly. Cast your nymph upstream with a short cast—no more than 30 to 35 feet. As soon as your line hits, you really have to mend hard upstream—almost a roll cast. You want to get as much of that line upstream of the leader as you can to get the fly bouncing down as close to the bottom as possible.

For most of my nymph fishing, I use the short-line, high-stick method of nymphing. After the cast and mend, raise the rod tip as the fly and indicator drift down toward you. When the indicator gets just opposite you in the current, the fly will be near the bottom, and this is where you will most likely get a strike. The strikes on a dead-drift can be subtle. If that indicator or line pauses the least bit in that drift, set the hook. High-sticking demands close attention to the line and indicator. As the indicator drifts past, then start to lower the rod tip and follow the indicator until the indicator and fly swing below you. You want to keep the fly bouncing on the bottom as long as possible, so, once it goes by you, start mending downstream or shaking any excess line out of your rod. Finally your line will start to straighten and swing below you. Now you're fishing the nymph in a classic wet-fly style. As the line straightens below you, the nymph rises off the bottom and the fish may take it for an emerging nymph. Some of us don't like to admit we catch fish on this swing, but it can be an effective way to complete your drift.

Pattern selection is not nearly as critical with nymphs as it is with dry flies. But I do have some favorites. I like to use my March Brown Nymph as an all-purpose nymph. Three other good patterns would be the Bead Head Prince Nymph, the Brown Bead Head Ostrich Twist Nymph, and the Pheasant Tail Nymph in sizes 10 through 14.

I am also partial to a plain Black Woolly Worm. I like it tied with a natural black hackle, black chenille, weighted well, in about a size 6. The Brook's Stone works really well. In fact any of the big dark stonefly patterns perform well because the river is loaded with big stoneflies. This is especially true just above Le Hardy Rapids.

Nymphs can also be effective in the shallower water. In fact, day in and day out, even in the shallower water, nymphs will be more productive than dry flies. The fish will feed on the insects before they start to emerge. By the time you see the hatch, the fish have already fed quite a bit on the insect. You can use the same tackle, but fish a smaller nymph, down to a size 14 or a size 16. I like a little Styrofoam indicator, something that you can attach to your leader, and actually slip down the leader and put where you want it. Set it up so you have 2 or 3 feet of leader below the indicator.

Most people aren't aware that, when you can wade the riffles and you can move up the channels, especially around Buffalo Ford, sight-fishing is often the most effective thing you can do. Instead of simply wading out and casting blind, stop and watch the bottom, and pick out fish to cast to. Not only is this often more productive, it is a lot more exciting than simple blind-cast, dead-drift nymph fishing.

Traditional streamers are more important in the Yellowstone River below the falls than above. In faster water, like this stretch on the lower end of the Black Canyon a few miles from Gardiner, cast slightly downstream so the fly doesn't move too quickly. Most fish are not going to expend the energy required to swim against a really fast current.

(Photo by Collin Brown)

Chapter 5

Streamers

Your streamer selection on the upper Yellowstone can be pretty simple. For early-season high water, carry a few non-lead jig heads in black or black and yellow with you. Take some Woolly Buggers which can be fished as streamers or as nymphs, some Muddlers, or some sort of bait-fish imitation that you particularly like. You have to fish something that you like. If you have faith in a Muddler, then that's the one to use. If you like a Zonker, use that. Fish what you trust.

In the Yellowstone above the falls, one of the most effective streamers you can use is a jig-head streamer. For years I really cringed when I heard the term *jig head* because it takes something out of the fly casting. It's more like casting a spark plug. But it can be deadly. And it will teach you timing on your back cast. If you don't let that line straighten behind you when you have a jig on, there's a fair chance it will cold-cock you on the forward cast.

The great virtue of the jig is that it gets down to the bottom of the river quickly. While we tend to think of jigs as heavy, spark plug–like flies, they can weigh just about anything, from really light to really heavy. On the Yellowstone, use jigs ranging from about 1/64 ounce through about 1/16 ounce.

My favorite jig pattern has a marabou wing, with black and yellow being my favorite colors. A good combination uses a darker color with a little flash of yellow or pink, or maybe a little Crystal Hair or Flashabou as an attractant.

Cast the jig across the deep channel, let it swing, and give it a little tip action, to make the head bob up and down. Many of the new bead-head nymphs, streamers, and Woolly Buggers will work quite well as a jig.

Above the falls, traditional streamers aren't as important as they might be on other rivers. But when you get below the falls, in the rougher water, there is a good population of sculpins and streamers do become important—in the Black Canyon area, especially.

There are two different ways to effectively fish sculpin patterns. My favorite way is to cast upstream, mend the line real well, and get it down deep. When I think it's down deep enough, I start stripping fast enough to get the fly moving and keep it moving, but not so fast as to pull it off the bottom. The other sculpin technique is to fish it in a dead-drift, like a nymph. Let it tumble down like it's dead or at the mercy of the current and trout will pick it up.

How you retrieve a streamer is often key to your success. Too often, people approach streamer fishing as a simple exercise of casting down and swinging across. While this approach has its place, it's not the only approach, or even the best approach. I have a rule. When I'm fishing fast water I tend to cast across and slightly downstream. The faster the water, the more downstream I'll cast so that the fly doesn't swim too fast. I try to strip the fly in slowly to make it look natural. In swift water, most fish are not going to swim really fast against the current, so I bring the fly in a little slower. On slow water, I cast upstream and across, mending, if necessary, to let the fly sink to or near the bottom. Then I strip the fly in quickly, and add some tip action.

The quick retrieve in slow water should imitate small fish. Small fish—whether a baby trout or small bait fish—dart. So I hold my rod tip down lower to the water with the line under my fingers and thumb like I normally fish, only I strip it in really quickly in short, maybe 8-inch jerks. On the really long, flat glides, if I want to speed the fly up some, I'll mend downstream to get a little longer and faster swing. By mending down, you increase the volume of line on the water. As the water current pulls on it and it gets taut, you get a big arc and that will accelerate your fly.

Fishing the Green Drake hatch in early August, yielded a typical cutthroat on a Jacklin's Green Drake Wulff just below Alum Creek.

CHAPTER 6

Mayflies
The Classic Insect on the Upper Yellowstone

When the season opens on the upper river on July 15, you can be almost overwhelmed by the number and variety of insects. But the trout do key on certain insects, and if you watch carefully, a few of the trout in certain areas along the Buffalo Ford feed on one specific insect. If you match that insect, you'll catch that fish.

PALE MORNING DUN (PMD)

The Pale Morning Dun, *Ephemerella inermis,* is one of the first and most important mayflies to hatch in the spring. Because the upper Yellowstone does not open for fishing until mid-July, in low-water years the PMD hatch starts early in the summer and is nearly over before the upper Yellowstone opens to fishing. In a normal runoff year, true to its name, it will start hatching about eight to nine o'clock in the morning during July and early August. The hatch is easy to match. The Pale Morning ComparaDun and a standard parachute in size 16 work well on the surface. For the emerger, the standard Pheasant Tail Nymph, trailed behind a dry fly, will cover most situations.

Western Green Drake

The Western Green Drake, *Drunella grandis*, is one of the legendary hatches in the greater Yellowstone area. One nice feature about fishing the upper Yellowstone is that you have a shot at Green Drakes around July 25 to August 10, much later than you will find it on other rivers in the region. If you want to chase the Green Drake hatch, go to a more silty stretch of the river. I like the area where the river comes out of the Hayden Valley but before it gets back to the highway again. You'll find a section of silty-bottomed and slower moving water that is really conducive to the Green Drake; they hatch there in droves. The most productive stage of the Green Drake hatch is when they emerge. I like to use the Green Drake Wulff in sizes 12 and 14, the Green Drake Natural Dun in size 12, the Slate/Olive Mess in size 12, and the Pistachio Cone in size 12.

Look for the most consistent Green Drake activity around mid-morning, but an afternoon cloud cover may sometimes trigger an emergence. Whenever the emergence starts, pay close attention to the rise forms. If apparently surface-feeding fish are ignoring your dry fly, they may be taking emergers just below the surface. If you see only a dorsal fin, and no snout on the rise forms, the fish are taking emergers. If you see the trout's snout break the surface first, then they're taking dry flies.

Gray Drake

On opening day, the Estuary can be especially good for the Gray Drake, *Siphlonurus occidentalis*. The Gray Drake is one of the great under-appreciated mayflies of the West. It's also one of the largest mayflies in the West.

When fishing the Gray Drake, you have to be really attentive to what both flies and fish are doing on the water. Pick out the individual insects on the water, watch their path and watch how the fish respond. Then duplicate that line. You can almost time a fish feeding to Gray Drakes. They rise at a certain interval. So time your cast so that your fly is the next one past the fish when he's ready to rise again and you can take that fish.

My favorite pattern for the Gray Drake is the Gray Wulff in a size 12 or a size 14. If things get a little tough and the fish are really picky, I might go to an Adams Parachute in a size 14. Or if they get a really picky, I might try an Adams Parachute on a size 16. Most days though, the Gray Wulff will work just fine. The nice thing about the Gray Wulff is that the wing will really stand out.

The Gray Drake spinner is very important. Toward the evening you get a good spinner fall. One of the best patterns for the spinner fall will be a standard Adams pattern tied in a semi-spent wing style on a size-12 hook. It's not a full spent wing and it's not an upright wing; it's semi-spent. The wings go out just like a B59 airplane, it lands on the water, it floats high, you can see it, and the trout take it without any hesitation. Another good pattern is the Gray Drake Para-Spin in sizes 10 and 12. The body color on this pattern is a creamy gray, and the tail should be forked. Don't miss this spinner fall. It can offer incredible fishing.

Small Western Red Quill

The Small Western Red Quill, *Rhithrogena undulata,* is probably the most prolific hatch of all the mayflies on the Yellowstone. You can count on it because it comes off at the same time every day from late July until almost the first of

August. If the weather is right, the Small Western Red Quill has a good midday hatch of duns and a really good spinner fall in the evening, so you can count catching it twice in a day. Concentrate your efforts immediately below fast water. The stretch below Le Hardy Rapids is a good one for this insect.

The hatches will be especially good on cloudy days. The duns will stay on the water just a little bit longer on a cloudy day to dry their wings, and that helps the fishing.

When the Red Quill is hatching, the best fly, day in and day out, is the standard Adams or the Adams Parachute in sizes 14 and 16. In the evenings during the spinner fall, the Rusty Para-Spin in sizes 14 and 16 is really effective. Although I rarely fish the emergers on this hatch because I love the dry-fly fishing so much, a standard size-16 Pheasant Tail Nymph is a reliable match for the emerger. If you decide to fish an emerger, tie it on to a tippet connected to your dry fly. This combination can be so effective that it almost seems unfair to the fish.

Small Western Green Drake

Coming into August, the weather continues to warm and the hatches start to become concentrated more in the morning and at dark. But you can still have good fishing on mayfly hatches. In particular, you'll start to see the Small Western Green Drake, *Drunella flavilinea*, also known as the "flav" hatch.

The flav looks like a cross between a small Green Drake and a large *Baetis*—olive, about a size 14. A size-14 or size-16 Olive Thorax works really well on this hatch. An olive parachute is also a good choice.

One of the best areas of the river to look for the flavs is the stretch above the Sulphur Caldron and below the islands at Buffalo Ford. This is the one stretch on the river where it can pay to wade deep. If you can get out to about waist deep and cast out across the trench you'll fish over good water, because the fish tend to stack up on that far side.

As with the Large Green Drake, I prefer to fish the flav hatch through the dun stage, and I don't spend much time with the spinners, nymphs, or emergers. If you're inclined to fish emergers, however, the size-14 Pistachio Cone is a sleeper all over the West on the flav hatch.

Blue-Winged Olive

The Blue-Winged Olive, *Baetis tricaudatus* and *Diphetor hageni*, comes out in midsummer. The midsummer emergence is really heavy on the Yellowstone River and it is especially good in late afternoon with a little cloud cover. It won't necessarily carpet the water the way *Baetis* hatches do on other waters, but you'll find pockets of water where the hatch is strong. If you find some fish or see a few flies, pretty soon fish will key on those flies and you can have a good hour or two of fishing just for that hatch in that one little isolated area.

Some of the most effective patterns include a standard Olive Thorax dry fly, the ComparaDun, or a Blue-Winged Olive Parachute. Fish either of these in a size 16 or size 18. I like to fish the *Baetis* dead-drift and I like to isolate a specific fish. As a rule, I'll try to fish from slightly upstream of the feeding fish.

As on other rivers, Blue-Winged Olive emerger and nymph patterns can be deadly on the upper Yellowstone. But my bias is toward the dry fly. As I said above, the Yellowstone is one of the finest dry-fly rivers in the world. And the cutthroat, a free and deliberate riser, is the perfect dry-fly fish. So, when I'm on the upper Yellowstone, I just hate to waste such wonderful dry-fly opportunity with nymphs and emergers. But, if you're determined to fish them, standard emerger and nymph patterns will serve you well.

The spinner phase of the *Baetis* has been mostly overlooked. But the *Baetis* has an unusual egg-laying activity that makes it attractive to fish. The female goes underwater to paste her eggs on the bottom. Oddly enough, when the female goes underwater, the male also goes under. This creates a "double" spinner fall, and the trout feed heavily on these submerged insects. The only fly design to imitate these insects is the Diving Blue-Winged Olive Egg Layer in size 16 or size 18. Fish it as a dropper behind a dry fly. Often, at the end of the hatch, this pattern provides fast fishing.

Tricos

During the morning in late summer, you'll see the Tricos, *Tricorythodes minutus*. You'll be fishing the spinner fall on this hatch, and it may be the toughest fishing you encounter on the upper Yellowstone. You'll need 5X or 6X tippet, and size-18 or smaller flies—Trico Para-Spin in sizes 18 and 20 is my favorite for the Trico hatch.

Casting accuracy is quite important here. You have to watch the fish feed and actually cast your fly right to the fish because it won't leave its feeding lane to come to your fly. Its rise line is really restricted. Often the best approach is from above, so you don't line the fish.

Here's an interesting variation on that upstream approach. Try to position yourself upstream and slightly across from the feeding fish. Make sure you have a long tippet. Using a bounce cast or a slack-line cast, drift your fly downstream, fly first, to where the fish is feeding. After the drift, let the fly swing out and away from the feeding station before you pick up and recast. This approach allows you to get the fly over the fish and make multiple casts without spooking it.

This angler plays a good fish in the slow, flat water of the Estuary using a Callibaetis *Para-Spin dry fly on a midsummer afternoon.*

Small Western Dark Hendrickson

In early September, the upper Yellowstone sees one more really good mayfly hatch—Small Western Dark Hendrickson, *Serratella tibialis.*

It's a midday hatch, and a size-16 standard Hendrickson dry fly or a size-16 Adams Parachute are both good flies to imitate this hatch. The Hendrickson hatch comes off intensely for one to two hours on the sections of the river with a gravelly bottom. If you hit it right, it can provide some great fishing.

Callibaetis

The *Callibaetis* is one of the great unsung mayfly hatches on the upper Yellowstone. Most people think of the *Callibaetis* as a still-water mayfly, and in fact, that's where you usually find it. It does show up on the Estuary below the lake during the early and mid-season, and can provide some phenomenal fishing.

Unlike their hold-and-feed behavior with most moving-water mayflies, the fish will cruise on the Estuary while feeding on the *Callibaetis*. Good patterns include a size-14 or size-16 Adams Parachute or *Callibaetis* Para-Spin, or a size-14 or size-16 Shroud. Sometimes they'll come to a Gray Wulff or the standard Adams, but when the fish are being fussy, the para-spin works best. You need to pay close attention to the surface during the *Callibaetis* hatch. When the fish are on the *Callibaetis*, they move up slowly and just sip the fly really lightly.

The *Callibaetis* is well-known as a still-water fly and you'll find good hatches of this fly on Yellowstone Lake in mid-July as well as on the Estuary. The fish might be on the dun or spinner simultaneously—both can be on the water at the same time. Late morning or midday is the best time to fish this hatch. When the fish are on the duns, use the size-14 Gray Wulff or size-14 standard Adams. When the spinners are present, go to the para-spin- or parachute-style flies.

Chapter 7

Caddisflies

A Good Bet All Season Long

There's nothing more frustrating than casting mayfly imitations over a fish that's feeding on caddisflies. At one time or other, we have all done this. Lacking anything else to go by, watch the rise forms. Fish rising to caddis will attack aggressively and splash the surface.

Once you can distinguish rise forms, you have to move from fish to fish. You must either change flies at each fish, or else you have to ignore any fish that's not feeding on what you're casting. But when they're on caddis, they may be on them from early in the morning, all day long, or just in the evening.

Early in the season, you'll find both the Little Tan Short-Horn Sedge (*Glossosoma traviatum* and *G. velona*) and the Little Plain Brown Sedge (*Lepidostoma veleda*) on the water. The Little Tan Short-Horn Sedge comes out of the fast water, the Little Plain Brown Sedge inhabits slower water, but you'll find their emergences overlapping each other. You can use nearly the same pattern for each of them. An Elk Hair Caddis is a good standard imitation. But one caution about fishing caddis hatches—lots of times we're fishing the dry fly when we should be fishing the emerging caddis itself. In my experience, most of the time when trout are feeding on caddis, they're feeding on emergers and not the dry fly.

While there are a variety of good emerger patterns out there today, probably still the best is the Emergent Sparkle Pupa, an extremely accurate imitation. Emergers work best right in the surface film. You want to grease the fly with some flotant. There's no hackle on it so it's flush, but you can see the wing right on the surface. It's a fairly visible pattern. Early in the hatch, before the fish are showing on the surface, you may want to fish a Deep Sparkle Pupa, which you fish just like a regular nymph on the bottom.

You can fish emergers two ways: either moving or dead-drift. You don't have to give it any wild action. The insect itself, while active, doesn't move wildly in the surface film. At times it will simply float in a dead-drift. Many times, however, a little movement helps. Use a hook cast, get the fly drifting into the fish, then give it a twitch. But timing is everything. You could twitch when the fly is 8 feet away from the fish and it does no good. The target fish won't even see the movement. You want to twitch just as it comes into his window of vision, which is generally about 30 to 45 degrees up from the trout's eye. That twitch alerts the fish that something is coming. On the other hand, you don't want to twitch right on top the fish. That may simply spook him. But once your line starts to tighten at the end of the drift, give it a twitch, and let the fly hang and bounce in the current some.

Remember, when trying to figure out a fish's range of vision while feeding, it will depend on how deep the fish is. The deeper the fish is below the surface, the larger his field of vision. If the fish is holding near the surface, its field of vision will be small.

Fish will also come up and take a dry caddis imitation. One of my favorite patterns is my Reverse-Wing or Fluttering Caddis with an olive-green body. You tie the deer hair tips in and cut the wing off behind the bend of the hook at a 45-degree angle. With a brown or gray hackle on the front that is clipped on the bottom, this pattern rides high in the water. Grease it up and it'll float real well.

The midsummer Grannom (*Brachycentrus* sp.) is one of the most common caddis you'll see on the upper Yellowstone. Their little four-sided cases will be all over the bottom. When the adults lay their eggs, they collapse on the surface, and they simply lie there. This is the best caddis to imitate with a dry fly, fished in a dead-drift. The Reverse Wing Caddis will certainly work well during this hatch, in a size 14 or size 16.

One other important tactic for fishing caddis is to fish larval imitations. Imitate both the cased caddis and the free-living caddis larva. Use a Cased Caddis Larva in sizes 8 through 16 to imitate the cased caddis. The free-living caddis are more abundant in the Yellowstone, virtually carpeting the rocks. They also drift heavily in the current. You can imitate them with LaFontaine's Free-Living Caddis Larva in sizes 8 through 16, or a plain dubbed green or green latex body with a little black head to imitate the worm.

Many important caddisfly species go underwater to lay their eggs, crawling or diving to the bottom. Both the females and the males enter the water, making this a double bonanza for the trout. The Diving Caddis, with an Antron body, imitates the egg-laying caddisfly. Fish this pattern either dead-drift or with a classic wet-fly swing.

The pupa is the most important caddis stage for the angler, because the fish gorge so heavily on the emerging insect during the hatch. Fish take the pupa when it is drifting deep, just after it has cut its way out of the pupal cocoon, and at the surface as they struggle to emerge.

You can imitate the insect at both levels, the bottom and the top. At the bottom, use the Deep Sparkle Pupa, fished dead-drift. At the surface, fish the Emergent Sparkle Pupa dead-drift. Both of these LaFontaine patterns, the first to incorporate Antron yarn into the design, are deadly.

Every once in a while, I will use a dropper. I use a size-16 plain green little pupa with a black head below a dry caddis imitation. Often the dropper fly will catch the biggest fish. The dropper rig allows you to cover both bases.

During midsummer, two common caddisflies are the Green Sedge, *Rhyacophila bifila*, and the Spotted Sedge, *Hydropsyche occidentalis*, and *H. oslari*. Both of them are about size 12 to 14. Even when they're not there in big numbers, they're always fluttering around all day long. Near dusk these caddis will come off in big numbers. Gary Borger's Poly Caddis is an especially good pattern for these hatches, especially on the Estuary. With the poly wing, you can give the fly a good twitch—actually pull it under the water—and it will pop back to the surface. When the caddis are fluttering and kicking, and the fish are cruising erratically and they're hard to time, you can pull them to the fly with that technique. Some other good patterns include large turkey-wing patterns such as the Henryville with a peacock body, the EZ2C Caddis, or the Goddard Caddis, well greased so you can twitch them and pull them under like the Poly Caddis.

Chapter 8

Stoneflies

If you were to look at any list of the great Salmon Fly rivers of the West, you wouldn't see the upper Yellowstone or Yellowstone Park on it. This is probably because it opens July 15. But it should be. We have great numbers of Salmon Flies (*Pteronarcys californica*) that hatch out in the Black Canyon and Grand Canyon of the Yellowstone. And by the time July 15 rolls around, these flies are also hatching out quite heavily around Buffalo Ford and Le Hardy Rapids. So if you're going to fish those areas around July 15, make sure you have a good supply of large Salmon Fly imitations with you. Think of the upper Yellowstone as having two distinct Salmon Fly hatches—one below Lower Falls, and one at Buffalo Ford and Le Hardy Rapids. The one below the Lower Falls starts outside the Park and moves through Black Canyon and into the Grand Canyon. As a rule, the Buffalo Ford hatch always seems to occur around the July 15 opening.

Salmon Fly patterns, including Jacklin's Giant Salmon Fly, are especially effective in the heavy water below Le Hardy Rapids.

For the dry-fly imitation Jacklin's Giant Salmon Fly, with a black egg sack and a bullet head works well. And big Salmon Fly nymphs such as the Brook's Stone, Black Woolly Worm, the Natural Drift Stonefly Nymph, or the Giant Salmon Fly Nymph will all work well fished dead-drift on the bottom. Remember—big and black is the key to these nymphs.

On sunny days, there are big hatches, especially at Le Hardy Rapids. As the females come on the water, the fish will concentrate on them.

Another important stonefly on the upper Yellowstone is the Golden Stone (*Calineuria californica*). No matter where you go in the West, the Golden Stone follows the Salmon Fly and the trout seem to like the Goldens better. They're a little smaller fly, a size 6 or even an 8. They're just a little lighter color than the big Salmon Fly. Their bodies are more tan with a hint of orange. The fish will key on these, so you want to have some patterns to imitate them. The Golden Stone is one of the most important insects in the riffled areas of the upper Yellowstone. It hatches just after the Salmon Fly, and there are more of them and the hatch lasts longer than the Salmon Fly hatch.

There is another big stonefly on the upper Yellowstone that is often confused with the Golden Stone, and that is the Giant Western Golden Stone (*Claassenia sabulosa*). It doesn't seem to be important on any other trout stream. People think it's the Golden Stone going all the way through the summer. But it's not. First of all, it's bigger. It's actually a size 4 or size 6. It gets the fish moving just like the Salmon Fly hatch. This fly will show up in sufficiently large numbers that it should easily qualify as a super hatch. Often, a Salmon Fly imitation will work just fine. Take a Salmon Fly imitation and skitter it over the deep water. Fish will come to it. This hatch can start up in late July or even August, long after the Salmon Fly and Golden Stones have hatched. So it pays to always have some Salmon Fly and Golden stonefly imitations with you. My Golden Stone Fly Nymph in sizes 6 through 10 works well on the bottom.

There are a couple of smaller species that show up in midsummer that are important—the Yellow Sally (*Isoperla* sp.) and the Little Olive (*Alloperla* sp.). The Yellow Sally has a yellow body and wing and it's about a size 12 to size 14. The Little Olive has a pale olive body and gray wing and it is about a size-14 to size-16 fly. You'll find these flies on the water in early to mid-August. An Elk Hair Caddis with the appropriate color body works fine for either of these. Another oddball LaFontaine pattern that works well on the Yellow Sally hatch is the Yellow or Olive Air Head in size 16. Also, bring a few of these patterns in sizes as small as size 18. If they won't come to size 14 or 16, they may come to an 18.

The shallows in the foreground, near Sulphur Caldron, once yielded a 22-inch cutthroat caught on a size-28 midge dry fly.

CHAPTER 9

Midges

iven the number of really good mayfly and caddis hatches, most anglers tend to ignore the midge hatches on the upper Yellowstone. That's a mistake. There are times when it can be really difficult to move fish during the better-known hatches. At those times, it's worth paying attention to midge activity.

The midges will appear in really specific spots. I tend to watch the back eddies near the banks, or other still-water or almost-dead-water areas. A lot of times at midday when there's nothing else going on, in late season, you'll see midge hatches in the still water if you watch really carefully. You'll see a little nose come up and just a really light little sip and maybe 20 feet away, another sip. The trout will cruise in the back-water areas, sipping on midges. You'll know they are midges, because they appear to be feeding on something that's not there. When you find this situation, you'll have to fish small flies, sizes 18 to 28, and a fine tippet of 6X.

I once caught a 22-inch cutthroat below Sulphur Caldron on a size-28 midge. I saw the fish sipping on something I couldn't see. It was feeding on midges, not more than three feet from shore, next to a large flat boulder. It took me over an hour on this fish to get him to take. There were thousands of naturals of the same size on the water. So, even when you have the right pattern and size, patience can often mean the difference between failure and success on midge hatches. One of my clients had the good fortune to catch this same fish from the same spot later in the season—on a size-14 Royal Wulff. So much for matching the hatch.

It's important to pay attention to the rise forms. If you see them rising, they're either taking the adult or they're taking the pupa. If the fish rises and you see its back come out, then it's taking the pupa just below the surface. And if it comes up and you see the nose, that's when it's taking the adult.

The midge patterns are simple. You don't need much more than a short black tail, maybe no body at all, and a black hackle trimmed down to a small size. A Griffith's Gnat is a good dry pattern. Another good standby is a gray midge pattern with a blue dun hackle and a short tail. If you don't have small enough hackle , just trim the hackle down to about a size 20. Or tie a size-20 fly on a size-18 hook.

For the midge emerger, a plain quill pattern with just a little dubbed head or even a poly head will work quite well. Another good midge imitation is the Halo Midge Emerger, in olive and black, sizes 18 through 24.

If you have to get deep with a midge (and sometimes you do), a brassy nymph with just plain copper or brass wire and a little black head works well, as does a Variegated Midge Larva in sizes 18 through 26.

Because these flies are so small, you have to really use tackle suited to this particular type of fishing. Which means maybe a lighter line and a finer tippet down to 6X. Maybe even a shorter, smaller rod. I'll use a four-weight rod with a 6X or even 7X tippet.

The small flies can be especially hard to see. Most of my midge fishing has been with a fairly short line, so I see the fish take the fly. You have to get close. In fact, that's the key to seeing any small pattern on the water and to fishing it effectively. I prefer to strip it in slowly. Just let the current take it. When the line tightens up, just lift the rod very easily. Midges are difficult to fish dead-drift, in part because they are so hard to see. You can improve your odds on the dead-drift if you use a small indicator close to the fly and watch that indicator.

The small fly and the refined tackle needed for midge fishing can cause special problems in approach and presentation. The best approach is from above and slightly to the side. You want the fly to drift into the fish before the line does.

The joy of fishing the Yellowstone is more than catching fish, it is the total experience. Bob Jacklin stalks a feeding cutthroat in the slack water of the Estuary.

JACKLIN'S CONCLUSION

f the good Lord gave me just one last day in which to fish, I would fish the upper Yellowstone River in Yellowstone National Park.

It has been my lucky privilege to fish and guide the last thirty-five years on the upper Yellowstone in the Park. For a trout-loving kid from New Jersey, it's been a dream come true. The opportunity to catch large wild native trout in a spectacular natural setting on one of the last free-flowing rivers in the lower forty-eight, is, for me, the essence of fly fishing. If you haven't fished the upper Yellowstone in the Park, you should. Whether you're a beginner or expert, the upper Yellowstone is about as close to heaven on earth as you can get. So come and fish the Yellowstone. You'll never forget it. Good fishing, and God bless.

Appendix 1

Hatch Chart

Caddisflies

Little Tan Short-Horn Sedge — *Glossosoma traviatum & G. velona*
Hook = 14–16, Body = greenish brown, Wing = tan to brown

Little Plain Brown Sedge — *Lepidostoma veleda*
Hook = 14–16, Body = brown, Wing = brown
Comments: Larvae especially abundant in backwater areas.

American Grannom — *Brachycentrus americanus*
Hook = 12–14, Body = green, Wing = brown
Comments: Concentrated morning emergences.

Green Sedge — *Rhyacophila bifila*
Hook = 12–14, Body = bright green, Wing = mottled gray/brown
Comments: Major caddisfly on summer evenings.

Spotted Sedge — *Hydropsyche occidentalis & H. oslari*
Hook = 10–12, Body = yellowish brown, Wing = tan to brown

Mayflies

Western Green Drake — *Drunella grandis*
Hook = 10–12, Body = dark olive, Wing = dark gray
Comments: Nymphs migrate from riffles to slow edges just before hatching. Mid-afternoon emergences heaviest on overcast or rainy days.

Dark Western Green Drake — *Drunella doddsi*
Hook = 12, Body = dark olive, Wing = dark gray
Comments: Prefers colder, fast-water sections of rivers.

Gray Drake — *Siphlonurus occidentalis*
Hook = 10, Body = grayish brown, Wing = gray
Comments: Spectacular hatches at lake outlet.

Small Western Red Quill — *Rhithrogena undulata*
Hook = 14, Body = reddish brown, Wing = medium gray

Pale Morning Dun — *Ephemerella inermis*
Hook = 18–20, Body = yellowish olive, Wing = light gray

Blue-Winged Olive — *Baetis tricaudatus & Diphetor hageni*
Hook = 18, Body = olive, Wing = dark gray
Comments: Hatch time dependent on emergence-pattern weather.

JULY	AUG	SEPT
••	•••	
••	•	
••	•	
•	••••	
	••••	••
••	••	
••		
••	•	
••	••	
••	••	
	N/A	

The weeks marked on this chart indicate the heavy hatch periods for each insect. The brief color and size descriptions of the adult stages will allow you to carry at least generally matching patterns.

Mayflies (cont.)

Small Western Green Drake — *Drunella flavilinea*
Hook = 14–16, Body = dark olive, Wing = dark gray
Comments: The great evening mayfly of August.

Small Western Dark Hendrickson — *Serratella tibialis*
Hook = 16, Body = dark reddish brown, Wing = brownish gray
Comments: Concentrated midday emergences.

Trico — *Tricorythodes minutus*
Hook = 20–22, Body = black, Wing (spinner) = clear

Stoneflies

Salmon Fly — *Pteronarcys californica*
Hook = 4–6, Body = orange, Wing = dark gray

Small Western Salmon Fly — *Pteronarcella badia*
Hook = 8–10, Body = orange, Wing = dark gray
Comments: Abundant enough to be important even during Salmon Fly hatch, especially just above Gardiner.

Golden Stone — *Calineuria californica*
Hook = 6–8, Body = light ginger, Wing = ginger

Yellow Sally — *Isoperla* species
Hook = 14–16, Body = yellow, Wing = straw yellow
Comments: Includes *I. mormona*, inspiration for classic wet fly, Mormon Girl.

Medium Olive Brown — *Isogenus* species
Hook = 12–14, Body = olive brown, Wing = gray
Comments: Found in slow, silty areas.

Giant Western Golden Stone — *Claassenia sabulosa*
Hook = 4–6, Body = ginger, Wing = ginger
Comments: Super hatch on upper river; creates midsummer frenzies not unlike Salmon Fly.

Little Olive — *Alloperla* species
Hook = 14–16, Body = pale olive, Wing = light gray
Comments: Overlapping emergences, as with *Isoperla* & *Isogenus*.

JULY	AUG	SEPT
	•••	
	••	••
	••	••••
••		
••		
••	•	
••	••••	
••	••••	
	••••	
	••	

APPENDIX 2

Popular Flies for the Yellowstone in the Park

Treat this list as a framework rather than a must-have set of flies. Work from it to fill your boxes during the winter, or if you don't tie, purchase a workable selection. You will not need all of these patterns at any given time or on any given section of the river. You can match how, when, and where you intend to fish to put together your own pattern list. Shops in the area sell most of these flies and many are available through mail order.

Should you bring favorite patterns from your home waters? Absolutely. A good fly will work anywhere. The same imitations and attractors that fool trout in the East, West, or South will take the rainbows and browns of the Yellowstone. At the same time, don't ignore the local killers-flies that have proven themselves on the river.

DRY FLIES

MAYFLY IMITATIONS

Parachute Dun 12–20
(Fools selective feeders; easy to see. In light olive, dark or light blue dun, cream, amber, black, and brown, this fly matches the major hatches. Emphasize the versatile Adams Parachute and the Trico Parachute for the Trico spinners and the Olive Parachute for the *Baetis* duns.)
Poly Spinner 12–22 (A more exact match than the parachute dry is often needed to fool sippers on flats. Carry rust, cream, and brown.)
Pale Morning Dun, ComparaDun and Parachute 14–16
Adams 12–16 (Important for late season *Callibaetis* duns.)
Blue-Winged Olive 16–18
(When the *Baetis* kick and flutter, standard tie often produces better.)
Rusty Para-Spin 16–18
***Callibaetis* Para-Spin** 14–16
Light Cahill 16–18
Quill Gordon 14–16
March Brown 12–16
Green Drake Wulff 10–12
Trico Para-Spin 18–20
Hendrickson 14–16
Olive ComparaDun 16–18
Red Quill 14–16
Gray Wulff 14–16 (To imitate the Gray Drake.)
Shroud 14–16

CADDISFLY IMITATIONS

Elk Hair Caddis 12–16 (With brown, yellow, tan, olive, and fluorescent green bodies. The latter also matches the ubiquitous small stoneflies.)
Fluttering Gray Caddis 14–16 (Also called Reverse-Wing Caddis)
Poly Caddis 14–16 (Pull it under and it bobs back up; it's deadly on the flats.)
Goddard Caddis 12–16 (all-black, all-white, and other standard colors)

DRY FLIES (CONT.)

STONEFLY IMITATIONS

Jacklin's Giant Salmon Fly 4
Jacklin's Golden Stone 6
Jacklin's Western Yellow Stone 8–10
Jacklin's Little Olive Stone 10–12
Jacklin's Fluorescent Green Stone 14–16
Yellow Sally 14–16 (Along with the Fluorescent Green Stimulator, a great general searching fly.)
Fluttering Stone 4–8 (A high-rider for twitching and skating during the Salmon Fly hatch.)
Bird's Stone 4–8 **Sofa Pillow** 4–8 **Flex-Stone** 6–8
(Tie these Salmon Fly imitations with dark wings and orange bodies in the larger sizes. The smaller Golden Stones need pale wings and yellow bodies in sizes 6–8. Carry in light-colored variations. A special stonefly, the Giant Western Golden, hatches on the upper Yellowstone in size 4, and even size 2. Its morning and evening flights during summer months create concentrated feeding. Use large, pale stonefly dry imitations.)

MIDGE IMITATIONS

Griffith's Gnat 16–24
(Heavy midge hatches in the evenings can baffle anglers. Griffith's Gnat is a good general dry fly, but during an emergence the trout ususally feed on pupae in the film. Then it's time for a pupa imitation instead of a surface fly.)

TERRESTRIAL IMITATIONS

Jacklin's Hopper 8–10
Dave's Hopper 6–12
Bob's Poly Ant 12–18
(brown, red, black, with looped poly wing for flying ants and termites)
Fur Ant 12–18 (brown, red, black)
Crowe Beetle 10–16
Looped Wing Flying Ant 14–16
Soft Black Fur Ant 14

HIGH-RIDING EXCITERS

Skating Spider 12–14 (cree, grizzly, black)

ATTRACTORS

Royal Trude 10–16
Lime Trude 10–16
Double Wing 8–16
Olive Wulff 10–16
Royal Wulff 10–14
Goofus Bug 12–16
Humpy 14–16
Air Head 16–18

NYMPHS

MAYFLY IMITATIONS

All Purpose Nymph 12–18 (cream, olive, black, brown)
Flat-Bodied Nymph 12–16 (Brown matches the squat *Rithrogena* mayflies prevalent in fast water. An excellent searching pattern in riffles.)
Jacklin's March Brown Nymph 10–14
Diving Blue-Winged Olive Egg Layer 16–18

NYMPHS (CONT.)

CADDISFLY IMITATIONS

Emergent Sparkle Pupa 10–20
(dark olive, dark gray, cream, rusty yellow, bright green)
Peeking Caddis 10–14
Diving Caddis 12–18
Cased Caddis Larva 8–16
Free-Living Caddis Larva 8–16

STONEFLY IMITATIONS

Brook's Stone 2–10 (light and dark)
Jacklin's Giant Salmon Fly Nymph 4
Natural Drift Stonefly Nymph 4–8

MIDGE IMITATIONS

Suspender Midge 10–14 (Tie in black, brown, green, and red with ethafoam thorax to make fly hang just under the surface.)
Variegated Midge Larva 18–26

GENERAL IMITATIONS

Hare's Ear 10–12
Pheasant Tail Nymph 12–18
Olive Pheasant Tail Nymph 14–20
Prince Nymph 10–16
Natural Black Woolly Worm 4–6
Bead Head Prince Nymph 10–16
Zug Bug 12–14
Blackfly Larva 18–20
Brassie 16–20 (Good when cutthroats grub in riffles.)
Black Woolly Worm 6–8 (Weighted for the lake.)

STREAMERS

Muddler 4–14
Homberg 6–10 (Fish wet on the lake.)
Marabou Jig 6–10 (1/8-ounce and 1/16-ounce; yellow/black, red/black, orange/green, red/green most popular)
Mickey Finn Bucktail 4–8
Black Woolly Bugger 4–8
Light Spruce 4–8

EMERGERS

MAYFIES

Soft Hackle, Olive and Partridge 14

CADDISFLIES

Deep Sparkle Pupa 6–20
Emergent Sparkle Pupa 6–20

MIDGES

Halo Midge Emerger 18–24

APPENDIX 3

Recipes for 27 Key Flies

Flies photographed by Doug O'looney

AIR HEAD, Yellow

HOOK TMC 101 (wide gap, ring eye dry fly), sizes 16–18
THREAD White
BODY Yellow mink fur or synthetic dubbing (dubbed rough)
WING Brown deer hair
HEAD Translucent, closed-cell foam

Also tie in **Olive** (brown deer hair wing/olive body).

BLACKFLY LARVA

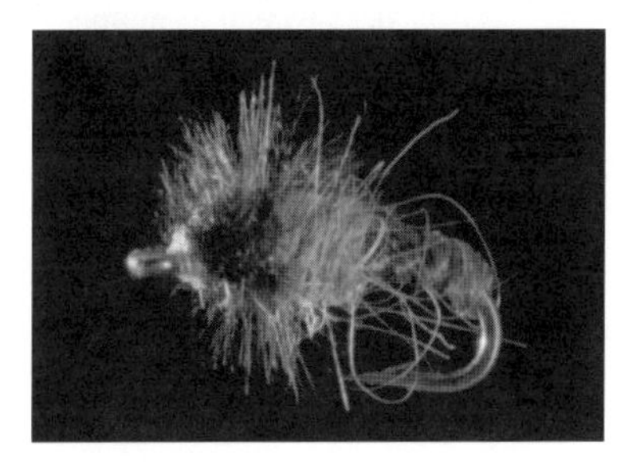

HOOK TMC 3761 (standard), 2X heavy nymph hook, sizes 18–20
THREAD Black
WEIGHT Fine non-lead wire
REAR BODY Dark olive floss (wrapped over back half of hook)
FRONT BODY Dark gray (dubbed over upper half of hook shank)
HEAD Black ostrich herl or marabou

BLUE-WINGED OLIVE COMPARADUN

HOOK TMC 9300, sizes 16–18
THREAD Olive, 6/0
TAIL Stiff natural blue dun fibers splayed over a ball of dubbing
BODY Olive dubbing
WING Doe whitetail deer hair tied in comparadun fashion
THORAX Olive dubbing
HEAD Olive dubbing

Deep Sparkle Pupa

Hook TMC 100 (standard dry fly), sizes 6–20
Thread Black
Weight Non-lead wire (optional)
Overbody Half sparkle yarn and half fur (chopped very fine and mixed in blender; touch dubbed sparse and fuzzy to the thread)
Wing pads Soft hackle fibers on each side of overbody

Also tie in brown/bright green, brown/yellow, light ginger (cream thread), and dark gray to cover 80 percent of the situations you may encounter.

Diving Blue-Winged Olive Egg Layer

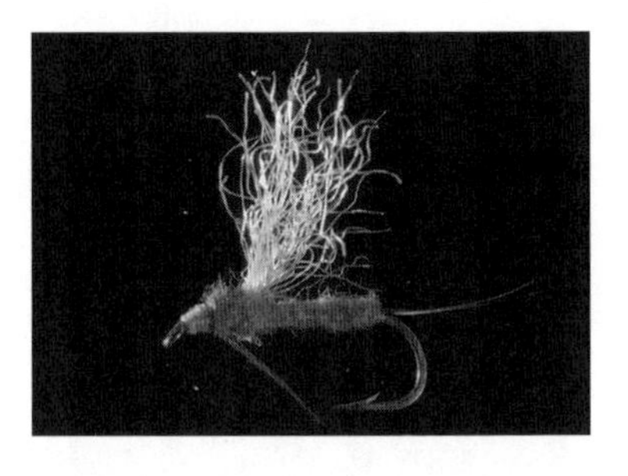

Hook Mustad 3906, sizes 16–18
Thread Olive, 8/0
Weight One strip of fine non-lead wire or bismuth wire under the thorax
Tails Medium dun hackle fibers
Abdomen Olive synthetic dubbing
Thorax Olive synthetic dubbing (thicker)
Wing Clear Antron fibers tied back at a 45-degree angle
Hackle Medium dun hackle fibers (beard style)

Diving Caddis

Hook TMC 9300 (standard wet fly), sizes 12–18
Thread Black
Rib Stripped hackle quill (for some color variations)
Body Half sparkle yarn and half fur (blended for color, dubbed)
Underwing Soft hackle fibers
Overwing Clear Antron fibers
Hackle Rooster hackle (low quality)

Tie in same colors as the Deep Sparkle Pupa.

Double Wing, Orange (use at sunrise and sunset and in autumn)

Hook TMC 100 (standard dry fly), sizes 8–16
Thread Black
Tail Burnt orange sparkle yarn stub (combed-out)
Tip White floss
Rear wing Brown elk hair
Body hackle Brown rooster (palmered and clipped flat top and bottom)
Body Burnt orange sparkle yarn (touch dubbed rough and fuzzy)
Front wing White calf tail
Hackle Grizzly

Also tie in **Lime** (lime green tail/white tip/lime green rear wing/olive grizzly body hackle/lime green body/white front wing/grizzly hackle) for midday and around green vegetation; **Gray** (dark gray tail/white tip/rust rear wing/cree body hackle/dark gray body/white front wing/grizzly hackle) for overcast days; **Yellow** (yellow tail/white tip/pale yellow rear wing/golden badger body hackle/yellow body/white front wing/grizzly hackle) for rainy conditions; **Royal** (green tail/red tip/brown rear wing/coachman brown body hackle/peacock herl body/white front wing/coachman brown hackle) for sunny days; **Pink Lady** (pink tail/white tip/gray rear wing, dark ginger body hackle/pink body/white front wing/dark ginger hackle) for early mornings and late afternoons; **White** (white tail, tip, rear wing/silver badger body hackle/white body, front wing/grizzly hackle) for shade, at dusk, or as a searcher.

Emergent Sparkle Pupa

Hook TMC 100 (standard dry fly), sizes 16–20
Thread Match fly color
Overbody Sparkle yarn
Underbody Half sparkle yarn and half fur (chopped fine for dubbing blend)
Wing Deer hair
Head Dubbed fur or wrapped marabou fibers

Tie in same colors as the Deep Sparkle Pupa.

Fluttering Gray Caddis

Hook TMC 9300, sizes 14–16
Thread Black or olive, 6/0
Body Gray or olive dubbing
Wing Reversed tied, dark gray deer hair
Hackle Medium blue dun
Antennas Optional

Flex Stone

Hook TMC 80B (flex hook), sizes 6–8
Thread Black
Tail Two rubber strands (tied split)
Body hackle Rooster hackle (palmered over the body and clipped)
Body Synthetic seal's fur (dubbed rough)
Legs Six rubber strands (three on each side; not overly long)
Wing Elk Hair
Head Balsa, deer hair, foam, or hackle of any color

The main colors are **Orange** (white rubber tail/brown legs/orange body hackle/brown elk hair body) and **Ginger** (yellow tail/dark ginger legs/cream body hackle/light tan elk hair body).

Free-Living Caddis Larva

Hook TMC 205BL (curved caddis larva hook), sizes 8–16
Thread Black

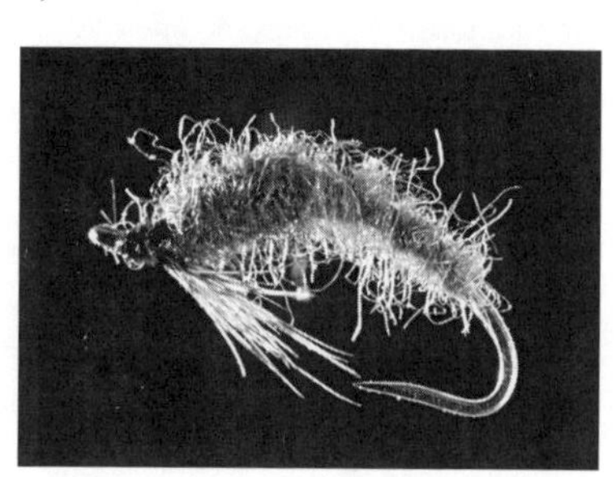

Weight Non-lead wire (optional)
Rib Light brown hackle quill (stripped)
Abdomen Half olive fur and half olive acrylic Craft Fur (mixed and dubbed)
Thorax Dark olive brown fur
Hackle Dark speckled grouse fibers (beard style)

Giant Salmon Fly – Jacklin's

Hook Dai-Riki 700 or 270, 4X long, sizes 4–6
Thread Gudebrod F77 Flo-orange, G

Tail None
Egg sack Black elk or deer hair
Body Salmon Fly orange dubbing or poly yarn
Ribbing Two brown saddle hackles
Wing Long blond elk hair
Head Dyed brown deer hair
Collar Dyed brown deer hair
Legs Four black round rubber legs, medium size

Giant Salmon Fly Nymph – Jacklin's

Hook	Dai-Riki 270, size 4
Weight	.020 non-lead wire
Thread	Gudebrod black, 3/0
Tail	Black turkey biots
Body	Bicycle tire tube
Wing cases	Bicycle tire tube
Legs	Bicycle tire tube
Thorax	Australian opossum fur dubbing
Eyes	Red mono, melted
Antennas	Dyed black pheasant tail fibers

Golden Stone – Jacklin's

Hook	Dai-Riki 700 or 270, 4X long, sizes 6–8
Thread	Rusty brown, 6/0
Egg sack	Dyed brown deer hair
Body	Golden Stone dubbing
Ribbing	Ginger saddle hackle
Wing	Light elk hair
Head	Elk hair dyed tan
Collar	Elk hair dyed tan
Legs	Four small black round rubber legs

Green Drake Wulff

Hook	Dai-Riki 730, size 12
Thread	Olive, 6/0
Body	Olive dubbing
Ribbing	Silk buttonhole thread
Wing	Black or dark dun calf tail
Hackle	Dyed yellow grizzly hackle

Halo Midge Emerger

Hook	TMC 900BL, 1X (fine wire barbless), sizes 18–24
Thread	Black
Body	Black or olive Antron touch dubbing
Halo	Large-cell closed foam
Spike	Orange deer hair

Jacklin's Hopper

Hook	Dai-Riki 700, 4X long, sizes 8–10
Thread	Yellow, 3/0
Egg sack	Coarse deer hair, dyed red
Body	Green poly yarn
Ribbing	Brown saddle hackle
Head	Blond elk hair
Collar	Blond elk hair
Head	Tied bullet-head fashion

Fluorescent Green Stone – Jacklin's

Hook	Dai-Riki 700 or 270, 4X long, sizes 14–16
Thread	Chartreuse, 6/0
Egg sack	Light gray natural deer hair
Body	Bright green dubbing
Ribbing	White hackle
Wing	Light elk hair
Head	Light deer hair
Collar	Light deer hair

Little Olive Stone

Hook Dai-Riki 700 or 270, 4X long, sizes 10–12
Thread Yellow, 6/0
Egg sack Light olive deer hair
Body Pale olive dubbing
Ribbing Light ginger hackle
Head Natural gray whitetail deer, dyed yellow
Collar Natural gray whitetail deer, dyed yellow
Legs None

March Brown Nymph – Jacklin's

Hook 1X long, sizes 10–14
Weight .020 non-lead wire

Thread Burnt orange, 3/0
Tail Three pheasant tail fibers
Body Australian opossum dubbing, muddy brown to natural amber
Ribbing Large flat nylon thread, dark brown
Wing case Dark turkey tail feather strip
Legs Hungarian partridge body feather
Thorax Australian opossum dubbing, same color as body, heavy and bushy
Head Australian opossum dubbing, same color as body

Natural Drift Stonefly Nymph

Hook TMC 5262, 2X heavy and 2X long nymph, sizes 4–8
Thread Black

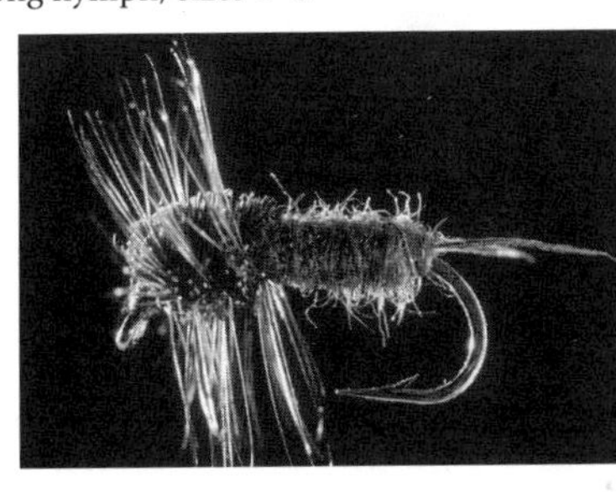

Weight Non-lead wire (over rear half of hook shank)
Tail Two pheasant tail or turkey feather fibers (split)
Rib Stripped brown hackle quill
Abdomen Dark brown fur (dubbed)
Thorax Black deer hair (spun)
Hackle Furnace rooster (palmered snugly through thorax hair)

Para-Spin, Trico or Rusty

Hook	TMC 9300, 1X long, sizes 16–20
Thread	Black, 6/0 or 8/0
Tail	Two Microfibbets
Body	Black beaver fur dubbing (or any fine dubbing). Rust dubbing for Rusty spinner.
Wing	Grizzly hackle
Post	Antron or poly yarn, white or hi-vis color
Thorax	Same as body
Head	Black tying thread

Pheasant Tail Nymph

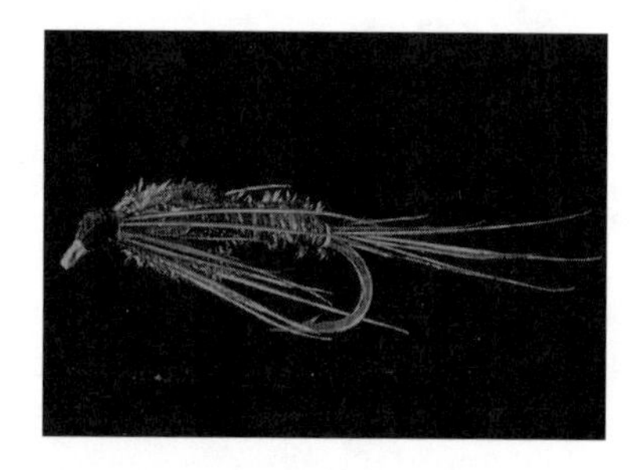

Hook	Dai-Riki 60, sizes 14–18
Thread	Black, 3/0
Tail	Cock pheasant tail fibers
Abdomen	Pheasant tail fibers
Ribbing	Fine gold wire
Thorax	Peacock herl
Wing case	Pheasant tail fibers
Legs	Pheasant tail fibers

Shroud

Hook	TMC 5230, 3X fine wire, sizes 14–16
Thread	Black
Tail	Red marabou
Body	Gray mink or muskrate fur (dubbed rough with guard hairs mixed into blend)
Hackle	Medium blue dun

Variegated Midge Larva

Hook TMC 9300 (standard wet fly), sizes 18–26
Thread Black
Body Two colors of marabou fibers and one long strand of clear Antron (spun in a dubbing loop)
Spike Tuft of white Antron (combed out, extending out over hook eye)

Western Yellow Stone – Jacklin's

Hook Dai-Riki 700 or 720, 4X long, sizes 8–12
Thread Yellow, 3/0 or 6/0
Egg sack Natural gray deer body hair
Body Pale yellow dubbing fur
Ribbing Light cream ginger hackle
Wing Light elk hair
Head Elk hair dyed pale yellow
Collar Elk hair dyed pale yellow
Legs Small pale yellow round rubber legs (optional)

Woolly Bugger – Jacklin's

Hook Dai-Riki 700, sizes 4–8
Weight .020 non-lead wire
Thread Black, 3/0
Tail Black marabou with flash
Body Black or peacock crystal chenille
Hackle Black saddle hackle

Appendix 4

Federation of Fly Fishers

The Federation of Fly Fishers (FFF) has been a large part of my life for more than thirty-five years. I was just twenty years old in 1965 and serving in the army when the FFF concept was born. It was organized to promote and protect and share with others the sport of fishing with the artificial fly. I joined the Federation in July 1967, becoming a charter member of what was then called the Federation of Fly Fishermen. I have been a continuous member and a life member of what is now called the Federation of Fly Fishers to include all people.

Please consider a membership in the Federation of Fly Fishers so you can, like me, enjoy learning about fly fishing, improve your fly-fishing ability, and share with others this great sport and way of life.

The following history and description of what the Federation is and what it does was prepared by L. C. "Bob" Burnham, past president of the Western Rocky Mountain Council of the Federation of Fly Fishers.

— Bob Jacklin
President, Western Rocky Mountain Council of the FFF

The Federation of Fly Fishers, founded in Eugene, Oregon, in 1965, was formed to give fly fishing a unified voice, to promote fly fishing as a method of angling, and to protect and expand fly-fishing opportunities. It is the only organized advocate for fly fishers on the national and regional level, and is now international in scope. By charter and inclination, the FFF is organized from the bottom up; each member club in North America and the world is a unique and self-directed group.

FFF works to maintain the fly-fishing opportunities available today—cold water, warm water, and saltwater—all fish in all waters. The organization also works to improve fly-fishing opportunities for tomorrow—actively working to restore and conserve clean waters and healthy ecosystems for all sport species. FFF believes that we need to protect all species and all fisheries habitat, and has encouraged catch and release of wild fish since 1965.

FFF provides a forum for the exchange of fly-fishing knowledge, skills, and techniques. FFF published the first fly-fishing magazine in the world: *Flyfisher*, today the journal of FFF activities, published four times per year. The FFF web page—www.fedflyfishers.org—is an award-winning source of information about FFF activities and programs.

FFF teaches the fly fishers of tomorrow the skills needed to be successful, supporting an energetic education program introducing children, as well as beginning fly fishers of all ages, to the allure of the sport.

The FFF also has a women's education program, having welcomed women's involvement in the organization for twenty-eight years.

The FFF's International Fly Fishing Center (IFFC), in Livingston, Montana, is a unique facility, housing both an outstanding museum of fly fishing and FFF's education center. The museum includes exhibits on the history of fly fishing, with displays of equipment, outstanding art, and flies tied by masters from around the world, and the Lewis A. Bell Memorial Fly Fishing Library that is available to visitors, writers, and researchers. The IFFC provides school programs, casting lessons, an equipment loan program, and a surface-water testing kit and teacher's guide for high school level students.

The All Fish, All Waters Foundation, Inc., is a nonprofit foundation that accepts tax-deductible donations to support conservation, education, youth, IFFC, and special programs of the FFF.

FFF started the Fly Casting Certification Program in 1992 for the purpose of enhancing the overall level of instruction in fly casting, including instructor knowledge, casting proficiency, and teaching ability to beginning and experienced fly casters.

For more information, contact: The Federation of Fly Fishers, P.O. Box 1595, Bozeman, MT 59771, phone (406) 585-7592. Also, visit the web site at http://www.fedflyfishers.org.

Suggested Reading

Books

Baughman, John. *The Most Complete Guide to Wyoming Fishing*. Cheyenne, Wyoming, 1993.

Hughes, David, and Rick Halele. *The Complete Book of Western Hatches: An Angler's Entomology and Fly Pattern Field Guide*. Portland, Oregon: Frank Amato Publications, 1981.

Knopp, Malcolm, and Robert Cormier. *Mayflies: A Trout Angler's Study of Trout Water Ephemeroptera*. Helena, Montana: Greycliff Publishing Company, 1997.

Kaufmann, Randall. *Patterns of the Umpqua Feather Merchants*. Glide, Oregon: Umpqua Feather Merchants, 1998.

LaBranche, George M. L. *The Dry Fly and Fast Water*. New Ed. Helena, Montana: Greycliff Publishing Company, 1998.

LaFontaine, Gary. *Caddisflies*. New York: Lyons, 1981.

———. *The Dry Fly, New Angles*. Helena, Montana: Greycliff Publishing Company, 1990.

———. *Trout Flies: Proven Patterns*. Helena, Montana: Greycliff Publishing Company, 1993.

———. *Fly Fishing the Mountain Lakes*. Helena, Montana: Greycliff Publishing Company, 1998.

Parks, Richard. *Fishing Yellowstone National Park*. Helena, Montana: Falcon Press, 1998.

Retallic, Ken. *Flyfisher's Guide to Wyoming: Including Grand Teton and Yellowstone National Parks*. Gallatin Gateway, Montana: Wilderness Adventures Press, 1998.

Schollmeyer, Jim. *Hatch Guide for Yellowstone Fishes*. Mechanicsburg, Pennsylvania: Stackpole Books, 1997.

Staples, Bruce. *Yellowstone Park*. River Journal Series. Portland, Oregon: Frank Amato Publications, 1996.

Travis, Tom, and Rod Walinchus. *Fly Fishing the Yellowstone River*. Boulder Colorado: Pruett Publishing Company, 1995.

Varley, John D., and Paul Schullery. *Freshwater Wilderness: Yellowstone Fishes and Their World*. Yellowstone National Park, Wyoming: Yellowstone Library and Museum Association, 1983.

———. *Yellowstone Fishes*. Mechanicsburg, Pennsylvania: Stackpole Books, 1998.

Audio Tape

Jacklin, Bob, and Gary LaFontaine. *Fly Fishing the Upper Yellowstone River in Yellowstone National Park*. Helena, Montana: Greycliff Publishing Company, 1987.

INDEX

About the Authors

Bob Jacklin

Bob Jacklin has outfitted and guided fly fishers in the greater Yellowstone area for more than thirty-two years and is a master fly tyer who has created many original fly patterns for the Yellowstone region. He is a FFF-certified master fly-casting instructor and won the coveted FFF 2000 Buz Buszek award for lifetime achievement in the art of fly tying. Bob lives in West Yellowstone, Montana, with his wife Sharyn and has owned and operated Jacklin's Fly Shop for nearly thirty years.

ary LaFontaine

Noted fly fisher and award-winning author Gary LaFontaine has fished the Yellowstone River in the Park for twenty-plus years. His other acclaimed books include *The Dry Fly: New Angles, Trout Flies: Proven Patterns,* and *Fly Fishing the Mountain Lakes,* and he has written innumerable magazine articles for fly-fishing publications. He was named Angler of the Year in 1996 by *Fly Rod & Reel.* He lives in Montana with his dogs, Chester and Zeb.